"I found ... that was the first time."

The "thing" was a howitzer shell he had recently bought at a miliary flea market. "[I was hitting her] two-handed, like a baseball bat," Joel said. "Sideways, up from the top, all different ways. I just lost control. I stopped when I got tired."

Only after he was finished and sure she was dead did he begin to panic.

"I remember running around, trying to turn the TV volume up, pulling the shades down," he said laughingly, as if recalling some spirited college high jinks. To his horror, Susie suddenly popped up on the couch in a last-ditch effort to save her life.

"She bit my finger, almost to the bone," said Joel. "Eventually I pinned her against something and she died. I'm not sure if it was strangulation or smothering."

It would be eighteen months before he took another life, but when he did, there would be no stopping him.

Joel Rifkin had finally found something he could do with conviction and expertise.

THE JOEL RIFKIN STORY

FROM THE MOUTH OF THE MONSTER

ROBERT MLADINICH

POCKET BOOKS

New York   London   Toronto   Sydney   Singapore

The sale of this book without its cover is unauthorized. If you purchased
this book without a cover, you should be aware that it was reported to
the publisher as "unsold and destroyed." Neither the author nor the
publisher has received payment for the sale of this "stripped book."

An *Original* Publication of POCKET BOOKS

POCKET BOOKS, a division of Simon & Schuster, Inc.
1230 Avenue of the Americas, New York, NY 10020

Copyright © 2001 by Robert Mladinich

All rights reserved, including the right to reproduce
this book or portions thereof in any form whatsoever.
For information address Pocket Books, 1230 Avenue
of the Americas, New York, NY 10020

ISBN: 0-7434-1152-8

First Pocket Books printing November 2001

10 9 8 7 6 5 4 3 2

POCKET and colophon are registered trademarks of
Simon & Schuster, Inc.

For information regarding special discounts for bulk purchases,
please contact Simon & Schuster Special Sales at 1-800-456-6798 or
business@simonandschuster.com

Front cover photos courtesy of New York Daily News

Printed in the U.S.A.

For my Gem and ACM

ACKNOWLEDGMENTS

THERE IS NO SHORTAGE OF PEOPLE who contributed in some way, small or large, to this book. To those who requested anonymity, you know who you are and I only hope you realize how grateful I am. To the others, I would like to thank them here:

Joel and Jeanne Rifkin for trusting me enough to share their thoughts and perspectives. Although the subject matter was grim and emotionally wrenching, I tried to be as fair and objective as humanly possible.

Bobby Cassidy Jr. for his invaluable assistance in gathering background information.

Bobby Cassidy Sr.—who was one of the best, if not *the* best, light-heavyweight boxers of any era to never win a world title—for making several introductory calls on my behalf to law enforcement officials.

Wally Levis and Richard Coffey for their brainstorming, patience, and enthusiasm in giving this book legs.

Chris Buck for his generosity.

Edelle James and Theresa Tobin for their logistical and moral support.

Tony Zon and Stan Berg, the superintendents of the Attica and Clinton Correctional Facilities respectively, as well as their staffs, for always displaying the utmost professionalism and courtesy.

John and Jean Maher (pseudonyms) for sharing their feelings on such a difficult subject.

Bill Shapiro, who as an editor at *Details* magazine in 1998 always said this story was big enough for a book. I will always be grateful for his advice, encouragement, and guidance in providing me with that springboard.

Charlie Stella, my friend and fellow writer, whose first novel, *Eddie's World*, will be published in December 2001. Charlie was like a tough workout partner throughout the often arduous months of writing. Not only did we read each other's manuscripts, we took each other's advice, laughed at each other's jokes, and helped navigate each other's path through this great personal journey. I am very grateful he was there for me, and wish him nothing but the best in his own literary endeavors.

Ray Pierce and Joe Piraino, who are not only two of the finest police officers I have ever met, but also two of the finest human beings. The contributions they made to this book were immense and I will be forever grateful for their graciousness, patience, and generosity. It was an honor to have them as colleagues, and it is an even greater honor to have them as friends.

Ann Kane for helping me gather the wherewithal to embark on a personal renaissance.

Teddy B. Blackburn for the friendship and spirit of camaraderie I will cherish forever.

Frances Haimeck-Mladinich, who inspired me to start writing again after a long hiatus. Although she departed this world much too early, she left a legacy of love that is as big as her smile was and will be in my heart forever.

My brother Charles, his wife Lisa, and their family for their strong arms of support.

My parents, Leon and Margot, not only for their enthusiasm and support, but also for opening their hearts and their home to my family when I was under crushing deadline obligations.

Giles Anderson, my literary agent, who was a constant source of encouragement, especially in the early going. He always insisted I challenge myself to find my range as a writer. He believed in me, as well as this book, even at times when I was so overwhelmed I had my doubts.

Thomas Hauser, the esteemed journalist and fellow member of the Boxing Writers Association of America. He introduced me to Giles, which set off the whole chain of events that led to this book being published. If not for him, it might still be just a jumble of ideas floating around in my head.

Mitchell Ivers and Amanda Ayers, my editors at Pocket. Having always been told that editors are a writer's worst enemy, I was thrilled to find that was simply not true. Their input and support made this a much better book than I could ever have imagined, and I am extremely grateful to have been able to work with them. Sometimes I think they know the book even better than I do.

I owe the greatest debt of all to my wife, Tiffany, who blessed me in more ways than I could ever have imagined. Not a day goes by that I don't thank God for having her in my life.

And, of course, Hobbs.

INTRODUCTION

WHEN I MET JOEL RIFKIN FOR THE FIRST
time, he had already attended the State University
of New York at Brockport for over a year. He was a
twenty-year-old transfer student and I was a
twenty-two-year-old junior who had just landed
my first paying writing gig with a now defunct national boxing magazine called *Hank Kaplan's
Worldwide Boxing Digest*. My assignment was to
cover Rocky Fratto, an undefeated junior middleweight who hailed from Geneva, in the nearby
Finger Lakes region. Fratto was battling a tough
journeyman named Steve "The Fighting School-
teacher" Michaelerya of Allentown, Pennsylvania,
at the Monroe County Dome Arena in Rochester,
New York, on October 26, 1979.

For the uninitiated it is hard to comprehend
just how popular boxing was at the time. Three
years earlier the film *Rocky* had won the Academy
Award for best picture of the year and spawned a
generation of fanatical boxing fans. Adding to the
fistic renaissance was the success of the United

States boxing team at the 1976 Olympic Games in Montreal. Not only did they win an unprecedented five gold medals, but one of those medalists, Sugar Ray Leonard, emerged as a bonafide superstar. The sport's newfound credibility and the widespread mania would go unabated for the better part of the next decade.

I had lied when I told Clay Teppenpaw, the magazine's associate editor, that I could photograph fights as well as I could write about them. In actuality, my only experience with a camera consisted of taking vacation photos with an old square Instamatic. When Teppenpaw asked for three photos to accompany a five-hundred-word story, I panicked. Just moments earlier, the thrill of being "on assignment" had been exhilarating. Now I was caught in a silly lie that threatened to end it all before it began. I immediately raced to the school's journalism department to see if they could recommend someone from the photography club to bail me out. Within an hour I was introduced to a rumpled, shaggy, and bespectacled transfer student, who, I was told, whiled away most of his days in the well-equipped photography lab. To my delight and relief, Joel had equally ambitious dreams of being a photojournalist and was as thrilled as I was to get a jump start on his career.

During the thirty-minute drive to Rochester, we quickly realized we had much in common. Although neither of us was particularly athletic, we were attending a school that was known most for its athletic excellence. We both hailed from Long Island and we were both quintessential loners who had long ago escaped into solitary pursuits, his being photography, mine writing. We were equally determined to make our mark as professional journalists and were not averse to doing so by unconventional means. Joel shared his hopes of taking up skydiving so he could make a living chronicling parachutists as they made their thrilling descents. I told him about my plans to spend the upcoming month-long Christmas break in the Albany, New York, training camp of "Gentleman" John Griffin, a political science major at Brockport who was putting himself through school by moonlighting as a professional middleweight boxer. With a record of four wins and no losses at the time, he would be training for a January 10, 1980, bout in Hartford, Connecticut. I was going to report on his whole month of preparation, as well as the actual fight, for a series of feature articles in the school newspaper, the *Stylus*. Joel Rifkin and I could not have gotten along better.

Because Michaelerya had lost a questionable decision to Fratto seven months earlier in Elmira, New York, he was determined not to let history repeat itself this time around. Never known as a particularly hard puncher, he stormed out of his corner in the first round and knocked Fratto down with a right hand that was launched like a rocket. Fratto managed to get to his feet but was immediately deposited back on the canvas with a flurry of punches. Michaelerya knocked Fratto down again in the second round and completely dominated him for the other eight. But when Fratto was announced the winner of a fight he so obviously lost, he seemed as shocked as each of the several thousand fans in attendance. Michaelerya erupted in anger, thrust his two middle fingers into the faces of the judges, and snarled, "If I knocked him out, would you have given me a fucking draw?"

The equally outraged fans began hurling chairs and debris through the air like confetti. Before long, chairs were six deep in the ring. Fistfights were breaking out all around as drunken members of the crowd tried to attack both Fratto and the officials. As a result Fratto had to be whisked away into his dressing room by security guards as fists, spit, and anything else that could be used as a projectile were flung in his direction. I was alternately taking notes, covering my head, and reveling in the excitement of it all. Joel initially sought refuge under the ring, but quickly realized that from a journalistic standpoint, valor took precedence over safety. He was soon amid the fray, firing away with his camera like a front-line war correspondent while bullets whizzed past his head. We could not believe our good fortune. On our very first paid assignment ever, we would not just be reporting the news, we were actually becoming part of it.

After twenty minutes of frenzied but intoxicating terror, we made our way into Fratto's dressing room. He had a robe bound tightly around his battered body, and his face was reduced to a mound of raw, lumpy flesh. Greeting visitors like a sickened Mafia don, he insisted he had legitimately won. But the look of hurt and dejection on his face could not hide his wounded heart. When I asked him if he felt dismayed by the sudden betrayal of his once stalwart fans, he pressed a swollen hand to his heart and throatily whispered, "Only here."

After trying to hustle some of Joel's photos into the city's two daily newspapers, we headed back to Brockport in the wee hours of the morning. Intoxicated by adrenaline, we talked non-stop during the ride. Neither of us could have imagined at the time what an enduring mark the evening would leave on both of us. Two decades later it would serve as both a metaphorical and figurative link between our past, present, and future, but on this night it was much simpler. For me, it would signify the day I realized with no uncertainty that I wanted to make my living as a journalist. Judging by the half smile that never left Joel's face, it was obvious that he was equally charged, not only by his immense grace under fire, but by the respect I was according him as a colleague.

Joel and I looked at the experience as a sign that we had found our true calling. We were both in our early twenties and neither of us had ever been particularly successful at anything before. Neither of us had brought any of the multitudes of other projects we initiated to completion because we were stymied by convention and terrified of being what we perceived as ordinary. That night offered a glimpse into our futures because we both subconsciously knew it would always serve as a dog-ear to our pasts.

I had been a cop for more than ten years when Joel was arrested in the early hours of June 28, 1993. He had been spotted driving his battered tan and black Mazda pickup truck, which bore a bumper sticker that read Sticks and Stones May Break My Bones, but Whips and Chains Excite Me, on the Southern State Parkway with no license plates. He then led New York State troopers and Nassau County police on a high-speed, twenty-minute chase through the highways and byways of Long Island. After crashing his vehicle into a wooden utility pole, police found the decomposing body of a once beautiful, petite twenty-two-year-old prostitute named Tiffany Bresciani wrapped snugly in a tarp in the bed of the truck.

He would later confess to picking her up in Manhattan several days earlier and strangling her after they had sex.

His account of Bresciani's murder was just a grisly portent of things to come. During intense questioning he would describe stuffing the bodies of prostitutes into fifty-five-gallon drums, enveloping their headless torsos in plastic tarps, and hurling body parts into makeshift graves all around the New York City metropolitan area. By the time he was done talking the body count stood at seventeen, and Rifkin was transformed from a seemingly harmless loner into the most prolific killer in New York State history.

Joel's first two victims were killed and dismembered eighteen months apart in his childhood home while his mother was away. Then there was Barbara Jacobs, thirty-one, whose body he stuffed into a plastic bag, then placed in a cardboard box and hurled into the Hudson River at West 10th Street in Greenwich Village; Mary Ellen DeLuca, a twenty-two-year-old native Long Islander whose father had been a former president of a Sons of Italy lodge; Yun Lee, thirty-one, whose body was crammed into a steamer trunk and dumped in the East River; a still unidentified woman whom he strangled shortly before Christmas in 1991; Lorraine Orvieto, twenty-eight, a onetime cheerleader who suffered from manic-depression and began using cocaine to control her mood swings; and Mary Ann Holloman, thirty-nine, whose last address was the Regina Residence Hotel, an East Village home to crack addicts and prostitutes. There was another still unidentified woman whose body he stuffed in an oil drum; Iris Sanchez, twenty-five, who had a crack habit, as well as an eight-year-old daughter and a sister who was a New York City housing cop; Anna Lopez, thirty-three, a mother of three with a fierce cocaine habit; Violet O'Neill, a sandy-haired twenty-one-year-old who was killed and dismembered in the bathtub of Joel's childhood home; Mary Catherine Williams, thirty-one, a high school homecoming queen and former cheerleader at the University of North Carolina; Jenny Soto, twenty-three, who had been in and out of detox and rehab for years, but kept returning to the sordid world of drugs and prostitution right up until the time of her untimely death; Leah Evans, the twenty-eight-year-old daughter of a Manhattan Civil Court judge; Lauren Marquez, a Tennessee native who had been raised in a military family but, consumed by drugs, took to the streets to support her habit; and, of course, Bresciani, who was his final victim.

When Joel's arrest set off widespread media coverage, I was working in a Brooklyn South squad, having been promoted to the rank of detective four years earlier. Although saddled with an overwhelming case load, I thought about contacting him then but was worried about impeding such a high-profile and emotionally charged case. Because I was so busy, I was surprised at how fast I got over the shock of his arrest once the initial jolt wore off. It was like reading the obituary of an old schoolmate. After recounting a handful of memories and taking a moment for introspection and reflection on my own life, I returned to the daily grind that prevented me from delving further into the case that would eventually consume me.

Five years later I saw Joel being interviewed on television by Geraldo Rivera and was appalled at the words that came out of his mouth. Although he talked about establishing a haven for the very type of women he killed, he looked Rivera squarely in the eye and said he felt no contrition for his actions. I wanted to hear him expound on that lack of remorse but Rivera launched into a monologue about how reprehensible Joel was. What seemed to be a golden opportunity to probe into the mind of a serial killer was wasted. I couldn't believe, as I stared at the television, that the kid I knew in college had become the person I saw before me.

From all that I knew about Joel, his early years were in many ways comparable to mine. Although he was adopted, we both grew up in seemingly normal, extremely liberal, two-parent suburban homes. Joel's father was a structural engineer, mine was a draftsman. Joel's mother was a one-time college art teacher and photography enthusiast who spent as many solitary hours in her darkroom as my father, also a photography buff, spent in his. Neither Joel nor I excelled academically, and both of us, as we realized on our ride into Rochester two decades earlier, were used to being on the outside looking in.

But mining that territory produced more questions than answers. Every child goes through awkward stages; every child gets taunted. If that is the criterion for someone to evolve into a serial killer, there is a talent pool of millions. Why him and not me, I pondered?

My curiosity finally got the best of me and I wrote to Joel in August 1998. I made it clear that I was an active member of the NYPD but was communicating with him solely as a journalist. It took four months and a follow-up letter to get a response. "I apologize for not responding sooner to your first letter," he wrote. "I get a fair amount of what I term psycho mail, fan mail, religious mail, requests for interviews and from wana [sic] be authors. I usually do not respond to any of it."

By the time Joel and I were reacquainted at the maximum-security Attica Correctional Facility in September 1999, we had exchanged numerous letters, but there was so much more I wanted to know. How could he so easily do something most anyone would be incapable of imagining, let alone completing? How did it feel for a mass murderer to be pen-palling with someone who is paid to put people in jail? Did the formative experience we shared so many years before have any type of lasting effect on him?

I never expected Joel to be as chillingly depraved as the fictional Hannibal Lecter or as charmingly manipulative as Ted Bundy—I expected to meet the same young man who had shared my hopes and dreams two decades earlier. With the exception of a pony tail, goatee, and an extra thirty pounds or so, most of which was centered around his gut, Joel had changed very little. "It could be fate," he mused when asked if he thought my re-emergence in his life was about more than just coincidence. "I am more of a fatalist than I am an optimist, but I think things happen for a reason. It has to do with that original meeting, your going to a boxing match and someone recommending me. I mean there were other photographers on the campus, other people in Rochester with a camera. You being both a writer and in law enforcement, I can see how you would be curious, so this to me makes sense."

What surprised me more than anything was that, given my vocation, Joel was willing to talk at all. "After we exchanged a few letters, I loosened up a bit," he explained. "If I were to tell any inmate in here that I'm doing a media interview with an active member of any type of force, be it a CO [correction officer] or just a security guard, they would be like you're out of your freaking mind. Not in those exact words, but I would have been cursed out and called a snitch and all these other things. Called insane, [be]cause there's a definite wall between [us]."

The reason he and I had no such wall had less to do with his having known me on the outside than with the fact that he had become a criminal after living twenty-nine years of a relatively crime-free life. "The guy who starts out in his juvenile years on the other side of the law, there's a huge wall," he explained. "Any CO in here will tell you that. They don't even know the inmate, and the inmate will get in their face and bark at them and call them all kinds of names and insult them just because they're in uniform. It has nothing to do with the personality. What makes me different than the average inmate is I didn't have this juvenile experience of being on the other side of the law."

As a cop I had sat across the interrogation table from a variety of criminals over the years, including murderers, rapists, armed robbers, wife batterers, and pedophiles. Several of my colleagues had even nicknamed me Father Bob for my ability to get perpetrators to talk. But my goal wasn't to hoodwink Joel. By virtue of my vocation I should have been predisposed to believe that all people, under certain circumstances, are capable of almost any crime. I had never been surprised by the actions of many other perpetrators, including several I had known personally throughout my own life. So why was I so surprised by Joel's? It seemed as if I was less concerned about coming face to face with a serial killer than I was with seeing someone from my own past.

But nothing could have prepared me for what I was about to hear. After twenty minutes of small talk, backtracking over the past twenty years, the conversation shifted effortlessly to murder and mayhem. Joel spoke with the emotional detachment of a man mowing his lawn as he described in graphic detail his descent from being a young man with dreams to a self-described sex addict whose lust for sex with prostitutes evolved into an even greater desire to kill them. He did not seem to receive any great pleasure from talking about it, but seemed more afraid I would lose interest in him if he didn't tell me what I wanted to hear.

True, many of his victims died while strung out on crack cocaine or heroin, dispirited by the sorrowful plight of their desperate lives, but Joel found it impossible to comprehend that they had once been someone's daughter, sister, mother, friend, or confidante. Through his own myopic, cynical view of the world, he never saw them as people, only as objects to be used for his own insatiable hungers and deviant desires.

"You justify things any way you can," he explained. "You just really warp things to justify what you have done. There is always a way of justifying, even armies justify what they do. Soldiers, when they are trained, [the enemy] become gooks, they become slags. They become not a human being."

Asked point blank what his victims were to him, his demeanor did not change a bit as he drew another wartime analogy. "They were an occupation," he explained unflinchingly. "I would forget any possibility of family, kids, parents, none of that. These were just objects. Like when you see a war movie and a guy blows up a tank. It is a tank, not a crew of five men in the tank. The same with shooting down a plane. It is a plane, not a pilot and a plane."

Although Joel spoke with the spine-tingling placidity of a Nazi death camp administrator describing his techniques to a rapt audience of bean-counting commanders, I found myself trying to imagine that I saw a searing desperation in his eyes, as if he too was wondering where it all went wrong. The concept of this once hopeful young man now being the personification of evil puzzled me greatly.

The idea for this book title came from the fact that, at one of his many sentencing hearings, Joel described himself as a "monster." As divergent as our worlds had become, I knew it was only because of our past history that I was given a chance to probe his mind. I vowed to him, as well as myself, to act like an impassive journalist and attempt to be as objective as humanly possible. I would provide a forum for Joel, and he would allow me to ask any question I wanted. Never could I have imagined that the task would become so mentally draining and emotionally wrenching. Even the most creative pulp writer would have been hard pressed to characterize the Joel I knew all those years before as anything other than a regular human being.

WHEN JEANNE GRANELLES MET BERNARD
Rifkin in the late forties, she was already considered
advanced by the standards of the day. While most of
her childhood friends settled for a conventional life
of domesticity, she had pursued a college education.
After meeting her husband, whom everyone called
Ben, she accompanied him to Oklahoma Agricul-
tural and Mechanical College, which is now called
Oklahoma State University. Jeanne took graduate
courses in education and eventually taught an art
class there. Ben received a degree in architectural
engineering.

Both of them were native New Yorkers, which is
where they settled after completing their studies
in the early fifties. They leased an apartment in
the Bronx and planned to start a family. In late

1958, when Jeanne was thirty-six and Ben was forty, they were approved for an adoption by the Louise Wise Services in Manhattan, an agency that specialized in placing Jewish children with Jewish families. Although Jeanne was not Jewish by birth, she had converted to Judaism after marrying Ben. Before long they were presented with a beautiful baby boy who had weighed eight pounds, six ounces when he was born three weeks earlier, on January 20, 1959. His biological mother was a twenty-year-old student; his father, a student as well as an army veteran, was her twenty-three-year-old boyfriend. The Rifkins named their bundle of joy Joel David.

As happy a time as it was, Ben felt great sadness over the fact that his mother had died less than a year earlier and missed meeting her first grandchild. But the happy family soon moved into a brand new home in Rockland County, a northern suburb of New York City that has since become a civil servant Mecca. Within two years they had adopted a second child, a girl born to different biological parents whom they named Jan. Rockland County was extremely rural back then and Joel remembers leading a Mark Twain-like existence that was mostly filled with happiness. Just before Joel started kindergarten, the family moved to East Meadow on Long Island after Ben landed a job with an architectural firm named Thompson and

Zark. The move would prove to be devastating to young Joel, who still refers to the times "before the move" and "after the move" as comparative periods of great joy and immense pain in his life.

"The happiest period of my life keeps going back to Rockland County," he explained. "The beginning of my conscious memory, when I was four, [we had] a very open backyard, maybe a half acre, surrounded by woods on both sides, across the street and behind us. So I had my frogs to play with, my tadpoles, and newts. Whatever crawled in the woods, that was my toy. That was before anybody [bullies] really started getting abusive. So that was a great time."

That was the one period of his life where Joel felt most unencumbered by neuroses. It was also, he recalls, the only time he ever felt like an accepted member of a group. "I remember the woods, the frog pond and that whole bit," he said. "I remember there was this drainage ditch. And I took my troop of friends and decided to go wandering down this drainage ditch. We saw a housing development down at the other end of this drainage ditch and we came back. We didn't know that we were gone for an hour or two, maybe three hours. We had every parent in the neighborhood freaking out. I was more confident back then, I guess. And I went to nursery school with the same bunch of kids, and I didn't have that many problems."

After the family moved to East Meadow in 1964, Joel's sense of impermanence grew more intense by the day. "Because of my birthday I had to wait a year to go to school," he recalled. "I didn't make the cutoff for the district, and there weren't that many kids my age. I went from having a lot of kids my age to practically none. The older kids would play stickball out on the curb, [but] I didn't have the coordination to join in. The only kid my age was my direct neighbor. They let him play all the time because he happened to be an athlete."

Things got even worse when Joel started kindergarten. Already feeling like a misfit because of his lack of both athletic ability and self-confidence, Joel had a host of learning disabilities that were beginning to surface. Besides suffering from undiagnosed dyslexia that impaired his ability to read, he would often stutter when beginning to speak, his mind would wander in mid-sentence, and it was difficult for him to follow simple instructions. Although it was later determined that he had an IQ well above average, many people meeting him for the first time believed that he was mentally impaired.

His feelings of inadequacy only intensified when he attracted the attention of a class bully who he believes dramatically changed the direction of his life. "[In] my kindergarten class there was one guy who would have been inside the [prison] system ahead of me, but he ended up killing himself in a motorcycle accident," said Joel. "He was completely out of control. Because of him I then had a reputation that invited other guys to join in. If you wanted to establish your rep[utation] as a tough guy, I was the guy you looked for. So I just created a nice little secret life for myself. I didn't hang out with other kids. I had very few friends."

Causing Joel even more grief were his always-growing feelings of incompetence around his father. A standout athlete, Ben tried futilely to get Joel involved in sports soon after he learned to walk. But like so many of their father-and-son activities, things did not work out the way either would have liked. "[My father] had been an athlete as a child," recalled Joel. "Had he had the grades under today's situation he would have been a college player in football. Those were the days when quarterbacks were more like running backs and you played both sides. No face mask and leather helmet type stuff. He wanted to take the baseball and the football out and play with his kid in the street. I had as much chance of catching the ball with my face as I did my hands. I was terrible."

Adding to Joel's woes was the fact that his next-door neighbor, a boy who was the same age as he, excelled at everything Joel didn't. By watching his success, Joel began to feel as if his own failures were continually rubbed in his face. To make matters worse, throughout their entire school career they almost always sat next to each other in home room because their last names were so close in alphabetical order. "He was the exact opposite of me," said Joel. "He could whack a Spaldeen [baseball] for ten hours straight, so he was always playing with the older kids. He was the athlete I wasn't. He was socially popular, I wasn't. He played with kids in the street, which I couldn't. He was president of the school. I went to Nassau Community [College], he went to Princeton. You know, the complete opposite. Total."

The dyslexia Joel suffered from was still a largely unrecognized condition in the sixties. His old-school father, who loved numbers almost as much as he loved sports, and was equally adept at both, would spend hours working with his son, but eventually grew infuriated at his inability to grasp the rudiments of math. "It irked him that he could do these crazy math things [and I could not]," said Joel. "These were back in the slide rule days. It took him a while to adapt to little hand-held calculators, [but] you could give him a nine-digit series and come back to him ten minutes later and he'd give it back to you. He could give it back to you backwards if you wanted. He could do mathematical equations and word problems in his head. Me,

I couldn't memorize a multiplication table. There would be many nights where he'd sit with me and we'd go over and over it and he'd get frustrated and have to walk away. He finally just gave up."

Ben's frustration only served to make Joel feel more and more like a colossal disappointment, the disenfranchised son of a man he perceived to be a genius. To their credit, neither parent ever slapped Joel with the onus of being adopted and they always thought of him as their son. They did not even tell him he was adopted until he was eleven years old. But even though Joel always assumed he was their biological son, he remembers being confused over the fact that he knew nothing of his family origins.

"Who am I? Where did I come from?" Joel said he used to ask himself in school. "The kids for a brief period were asking what time they were born, when they were born, what their ethnicity was. Either I made it up, or I just said I didn't know. And again I was like the odd man out because I didn't have the knowledge."

Had he been placed in special education early on, Joel believes his emotional growth would not have been so severely stunted. "Dad was actively going to the school and talking to the principals and administrators, [but] the sixties really weren't set up [for children with special needs]," he said. "There would be a special classroom for [grades] six through twelve for what were called the odd-balls. [Maybe] I wouldn't have been diagnosed as dyslexic in my twenties. I would have been diagnosed earlier, probably [in my] pre-teens."

While many children grow up surrounded by a close-knit group of friends, Joel, traumatized by the move, the persistent assaults of his tormentor, and his feelings of inferiority around his father, developed a serious social anxiety disorder. Although he yearned to be accepted by others, he was most comfortable alone. He began hiding himself in places where he could not be found and developing a fantasy life that lasted well into adulthood. He remembers telling his first-grade teacher that he wanted to write a book, even though his dyslexia caused an array of embarrassing problems with both reading and writing. Writing was the only endeavor he could think of that would allow him always to be alone.

"Joel always wanted to please my husband, but could never find a way to do it," said Jeanne. "I thought of him as a loner, it didn't fully come home to me what was happening until later. Joel would sit on the curb to play ball with the other kids, but they wouldn't let him play. He would then retreat upstairs and watch out the window."

Jeanne desperately wanted to approach the insensitive kids and demand that they include her son in their games, but she knew that would only add to the grief he was already experiencing. "How [could] I go to the kids and say let him play?" she wondered. "He would never be able to live that down."

At that stage of his life, Joel differed greatly from his sister who was much more socially adjusted, had a good group of emotionally healthy friends and, according to her mother, was more adept at gauging other people's feelings toward her. Jeanne felt Joel was unable to interpret the facial expressions and body language of others. "He never seemed to be aware that people were angry or annoyed with him," said Jeanne. "[He] would do anything for attention, even if it was negative attention."

For all of his problems, Joel was able to derive joy early on from horticulture and photography, solitary pursuits that were also two of his mother's favorite hobbies. "With gardening, he was right in there," Jeanne recalled. "For a kid who couldn't spell, he could remember all the Latin names of plants. One time at the Museum of Natural History, Joel could spell them all in Latin, but not in English. He also loved to disperse seeds throughout the yard, as well as anything to do with fossils."

In an eerie prelude to his obsession with accumulating souvenirs from his victims, Joel became a compulsive collector. As young as six years old, he would excitedly anticipate rock and fossil expeditions, where he unearthed, among other things, chalk, clay, coal, coral, sandstone, limestone, and basalt. All of these items were proudly showcased in his room, giving a visitor the impression that he wanted to be an archaeologist or a professor someday.

Jeanne was even more ecstatic when her son developed an interest in photography. "It was thrilling for me, absolutely," she recalled. "And I used to let him use the dark room, even encouraged him to use it, and he has never been the neatest person. He had a great eye for composition and was good at so many things, but never took anything far enough. He was great at starting things, but never finishing them. I couldn't understand why."

Although Joel had much more in common with his mother, his most profound familial memories concern his father. He saw him as a mountain of a man who could hold his own in any physical, social, or intellectual arena. He also saw him as a man he could never make proud and whose legacy he could never live up to. His face distorts into a childish yet hurtful grin when describing his father's exploits on the battlefield during World War II, or on the college gridiron during an era when helmets were not routinely worn. In the early seventies Ben had been the vice president of the East Meadow school board, as well as a trustee of the town's public library, where a sunlit atrium is dedicated to him. By all accounts, especially those of his son, he was revered by all who knew him.

Joel always believed that his father, although somewhat modest, basked in the adulation he received as much as the goodwill he dispensed. "He could walk into a room and light it up," he recalled. "He was very gregarious, I guess that's the word, [always giving] big hugs and pats on the back." Oddly enough, one of the things Joel always admired about Ben was his refusal to glorify violence, even though he had experienced plenty of it during World War II. While many of Ben's more macho friends regularly regaled an impressionable Joel with tales of bloodshed on the battlefield, the killer-to-be actually worshiped his father for not trying to get mileage out of his days as a foot soldier in the European theater.

"I know guys who were World War II veterans [who would go] to the VFW, sit around, kick back, and tell stories of the war like that was the only time they felt alive," said Joel. "And Dad would never talk about the war. Even as a kid, [I would say] 'Daddy, tell me a story.' His war stories were all non-combat stories. He never told me about all the kids [young GIs] he saw getting blown up."

Ben's favorite story was the one when he, a sergeant, and his driver were going through a short tunnel when they encountered another vehicle coming in the opposite direction. As they crossed paths, the occupants of both Jeeps—one German, one American—realized they had just passed the enemy. "They all did double-takes and kept going," laughed Joel. "No one became a hero and turned around and chased. They were like 'oh no, damn,' and they kept going. He [didn't] tell stories about the blood and guts stuff."

The fact that Ben distanced himself from the violence he bore witness to as a young, impressionable soldier, even while living in a suburban culture where it might have served him well, was a noble effort to shield his always curious son from the atrocities of war. The fact is he and Jeanne went to great lengths to help Joel adjust to a world he felt so uncomfortable in. They always assisted him with his schoolwork and never missed a meeting with his teachers. Even though they came from a generation that frowned on psychiatry, they brought Joel to a doctor in the hope of learning the origin of his dysfunctions.

Because they had a stable, loving marriage, mingled well in social circles, and had many significant friendships, Joel's behavioral patterns confounded them. Making things more confusing was the fact that Jan was so well adjusted. Although Joel was unable to articulate it to himself as a youngster, he was very aware of his parents' innate decency. But that didn't prevent him from experiencing conflicting emotions over his relationship with his father. As much as he and Ben had battled over the years, there was an intricate link between them. Knowing how proud his father always wanted to be of him, and what a bitter disappointment he had actually become, caused Joel even more heartache. His entire life had been a series of enthusiastic starts and premature stops. And, as well intentioned as his father was, he never let him forget that.

ALTHOUGH JOEL'S PARENTS WERE WELL aware of his adjustment problems, they were oblivious of the degree of abuse their son endured at the hands of others. Jeanne remembers only one time when Joel came home from elementary school visibly upset. He was in the fourth or fifth grade. "He was red in the face and said he had been waylaid on the way home," she recalled. "The kids pulled his underwear off. My husband wanted to go to the school, but Joel begged him not to. My husband took care of it [by talking to the parents of the bullies] and that group never bothered Joel again."

While that group might not have bothered him again, there were plenty of others to take their place. Joel devised a surefire strategy to avoid his confrontational classmates, but it only sent him deeper into his own little world. "The [school] building formed an **H** and there were two entrances with a walkway across," he said. "We had to line up and our line went this way and the older kids' line went that way. I used to be terrified to get on the line. So I used to time it so I would walk up the block as everyone was going in. I'd get later and later, then start walking in a few minutes late."

Although now safe from his tormentors for at least a few hours, he would immediately begin worrying about how to get home safely. "In grade school there is not much to do, but I [would] clean the fish tank [in the principal's office], clean the erasers, whatever," to stay in the school long after all the other students went home. What Joel was learning to do better than anything else was to outfox others as a means of self-preservation. That type of cunning would benefit him greatly later on, as he managed to remain an invisible but deadly force during his four-year bloodbath.

What is so ironic about this point in Joel's young life is the fact that he developed two habits that played critical roles in his future actions as a killer. His obsessive thinking was spawned during the seemingly endless hours waiting for the final bell to ring at school, and his strategic planning on how to get in and out of school safely laid the foundation for his ability to avoid detection for so long.

The gym was the one place in school where Joel could not hide, so physical education class was pure hell for him. "You had to have four years of gym in high school," he said. "If you weren't athletic it was a total waste and you were set up for abuse. They didn't have a gym for misfits. We went there with the football players. Now I think they're more sensitive than that."

Not wanting to be different from his peers at first, Joel tried desperately to fit in by attempting some of the sports his father had exposed him to. But he failed at every endeavor, subjecting himself to even more ridicule in the process. To compensate for being such a social and athletic failure, he tried to save face by showing others he was choosing his own path. By daring to be different, Joel believes he might have been subconsciously setting himself up for abuse all those years.

"I would do things to antagonize the problem," he explained, as if blaming himself, an altogether different stance from the one he would take when describing who and what was to blame for his murders. "Now kids use backpacks. I started out with my grandfather's backpack. It started to fall apart, so I switched to a suitcase of all stupid things. I'm walking around with a little brown and tan suitcase. I ran for student body vice president in junior high school. I guess I wanted attention. I mean the whole election was a popularity contest. I think I got twenty votes, or something like that."

He also took elective violin lessons, even though drums were all the rage. "So here I am walking around with a violin case, and you just don't walk around as a guy with a violin case in school if you [don't] want to attract all the [bullies] of the world," he said.

Joel joined the track team in high school and hoped that by doing so he could erase many of his past humiliations, as well as garner some much-desired appreciation from his father and his peers. He also viewed it as a means of self-preservation, thinking once he became a member of a team or fraternity, his inclusion in that elite clique would at the very least preclude him from being abused by outsiders. "I learned if you fought back you got beaten worse," he said. "I'd take the public pummeling, go down, the guy would be satisfied, his manhood intact. I knew who my enemies were because they were all on the track team. If you join a gang [or team], then no one else can touch you."

Things started off fine and Joel enjoyed what he thought was a brief period of comfort and camaraderie among his teammates. But as in so many other instances where he dared to be "normal," it did not take long for things to disintegrate badly. Getting his head dunked into a toilet bowl or a dead chicken stuffed in his mouth were just some of the things he endured. At one point he developed what he thought was a mutually caring relationship with a sensitive female teammate. However, her older brother, the star of the team, did not share his sister's sensitivity and decided to have a little fun at Joel's expense.

"I stopped by the house to pick her up once," he recalled. "Big brother decides to do the old check-out-the-boyfriend routine, even though he knows me from the team. So while he is asking twenty-one questions, he is cleaning a shotgun. He is rubbing it and brushing it, the whole bit."

Joel gulped hard when the boy, trying his best to sound like a man with genuine paternal concerns, said, "Don't hurt my sister," as he clicked and pumped the weapon for the utmost dramatic effect. "I was like 'gee, nice and subtle message,'" recounted Joel laughingly, although he is the first to admit he wasn't laughing at the time.

Once the rest of the team got wind of the relationship, the games really began. One day Joel was working hard at his part-time job at the public library and was eagerly looking forward to meeting his girlfriend afterward. Shortly before the end of his shift a group of teammates, armed with eggs and shaving cream, converged on the building and immediately blocked all the exits. While Joel had come to expect such incidents, he still couldn't help feeling deflated and dismayed. Just as he had begun to enjoy a newfound sense of security, he found himself facing the most painful betrayal of all. Like a cornered rabbit, his heart beating wildly, his eyes dashing furtively about, he realized he had to make a quick decision. Should he step outside and take his physical and verbal assault like a man? Or should he take the path of least resistance and run? He chose the latter.

"I decided to just have Dad pick me up, which was like a big sissy mistake," he says despairingly, as if still shouldering the ignominy of the experience a quarter of a century later. What was even more hurtful than the incident itself was the fact that his girlfriend, urged on by the crowd, was laughing heartily along with them. "I don't know if the whole thing with her from the beginning, day one, was a setup, or if it developed later on," he lamented.

Joel escaped the perils of the library in the safety of the family automobile, but not before his tormentors filled his gym bag with eggs and shaving cream. Having witnessed so many similar occurrences, his father was unmoved. "By that time, it was normal," said Joel. "He gave up trying. In grade school, up until a little of junior high school, he used to want to know who the kid was [who bullied me] and he would go talk to the father. A couple of times [it would help], but [mostly] it would encourage it."

Joel got to the point where he could take nothing at face value. While at a teenage leadership retreat at summer camp, he took advantage of the fact that nobody knew his personal history and began boasting about how easy it was to ask someone for a date. Before he knew it, he found himself dared into doing just that. Much to his surprise the girl happily agreed and the two went to see a movie, then planned to attend a party for their second date. While riding their bicycles to the party, the always fearful Joel, thinking a setup awaited him, began to panic. Terrified of being humiliated in front of a girl he actually liked, and who seemed to like him in return, he adamantly refused to attend, even though they had pedaled to within yards of the house. A fumbling Joel painstakingly told her about the bet, but to this day does not know whether it was a setup or not because he never mustered enough courage to go inside the house.

"She thought the whole date was a setup to use her," he recalled. "So she took it very badly and I had no idea how to deal with it. But she had told her girlfriends that I had made the bet, and it was just a total disaster."

Still, Joel did not learn his lesson. At a party one night during the school year, he downed a few beers in order to loosen up and fit in. "I don't know if it trashed my judgment or what, but we started playing the game of who do you have a crush on. And I make the mistake of telling the truth. There was this girl who was in all of the school plays. I sat in the row behind her in biology class, and I had this basic schoolboy crush on the girl. And she knew it, but she was dating some guy from a different school so we just talked. I took her picture a few times for the yearbook, that kind of thing."

During the winter track season, Joel and his teammates were running in the building because it was snowy and muddy outside. As they completed the first circuit, they ran past the girl's locker and there was a collective giggle from his teammates. Still unaware of what was transpiring but his radar on high alert, Joel felt his palms begin to sweat and his chest begin to tighten. He experienced a tremendous sense of relief as the group ran past the locker and through much of the next circuit without incident. Suddenly the murmurings grew louder as the group approached the girl's locker for the second time. Although their words were undecipherable, Joel knew he was about to become either the butt of a joke or the victim of some type of assault.

"I end up being pinned [against the girl's locker] by one of the shot-putters," he said unflinchingly. "And they take out this big, huge one-inch magic marker, the graffiti type, and just covered the whole thing [with] her name, my name, a lot of four-letter words, a lot of basic sexual remarks."

After practice ended, a mortified Joel was determined to clean the girl's locker in order to spare her any humiliation. Why should she suffer because the class geek had a powerful crush on her? He located a custodian who supplied him with a foam cleaner that removed all the graffiti from the locker. Although he was certain she would not have noticed anything awry the next day, he took the liberty of calling her at home that night in the unlikely event the culprits performed a similar assault on her locker in the morning.

"I never called her before, she never gave me her phone number, but I found it in the phone book and I explained the whole thing to her," he recalled. "I said I just wanted to let you know, in case they come in early and do something. They were never brazen enough to do it in public, so there was no repeat of the incident. But I was seriously mad, and it takes a lot to get me mad."

The girl seemed somewhat embarrassed, but did not take Joel to task for what had happened. She thanked him for calling, and told him things were still okay between them. As humiliated as Joel was, for one of the only times in his life he liked the sense of power he derived from his unbridled anger. "I went on a little hunting party the next couple of days," he remembered enthusiastically. "Basically, I found some of the guys who had done it and we got into a yelling match and a couple of them got pushed up against lockers. [I] basically [said], 'you guys might be able to knock me out, hospitalize me, but I am going to hurt you.'"

Joel's anger was sated after his uncharacteristically aggressive response, and he was unable to maintain any momentum after exacting his "revenge." He soon fell back into playing the role of a hapless victim. He couldn't even give himself credit for acting like a "man" for one of the few times in his life. After the locker incident he quit the team and retreated back into his self-imposed isolation. But on a deeper level he was always happy with himself for standing up to the tyrants. "It was like the only time I did something like that, where I took an affirmative, defensive step," he said.

One has to wonder if Joel yearned to recreate those fleeting feelings of power when killing his victims, though Joel's mother finds that theory difficult to fathom. As much of an outcast as Joel had become, she insists that he never exhibited any antisocial behavior. Not once did she remember him striking back at anyone less formidable than himself, going on destructive binges, or misbehaving in school. "That is why so much of this makes no sense," she said. "In hindsight there should be some evidence of crazy behavior. There is none. I can't believe you just start killing people without building up to it. Usually, in hindsight, it is easy to understand things like this. But with Joel, it's like putting a square peg into a round hole."

What Jeanne did not know was that Joel had been entertaining graphic and violent sexual fantasies since his childhood. They were diverse—from having sex slaves and captives to harming women with pointed objects like darts and arrows to killing the captain of the track team. "There was some bondage, there was some rape," said Joel. "There was a gladiator type thing with two girls that would fight each other until the death." He admits that he often harmed the women in the fantasies, but said there was always "no screaming, [they were] just passive about it. Everybody has some kind of fantasy life, whether it's positive or negative. [But it never got] to a point where it took over my day and became an all-encompassing obsession. It was a fleeting thing. And there were other fleeting things that were much more positive."

By junior high school his most recurring sexual fantasy was the scene of a woman being strangled in *Frenzy*, a 1972 film directed by Alfred Hitchcock. The victim is a well-endowed secretary at a dating service who is strangled with a necktie after rebuffing the advances of a well-dressed, deceptively urbane, maniacal client. In typical Hitchcock fashion his camera closes in on the terror in the victim's desperate, pleading eyes as the life is snuffed out of her.

Little did his mother—or Joel for that matter—know what a role these fantasies would play later in Joel's life, or the horrible consequences that would occur as a result of them.

DURING JOEL'S SENIOR YEAR OF HIGH
school, in 1977, his mother remembers an incident that left an indelible mark on both her and
Joel's psyches. As a member of the yearbook com-
mittee, Joel was put in charge of taking most of
the photos for the book. She was thrilled for him
because she believed he might finally garner acceptance from his classmates. He took his job
much more seriously than most of the other com-
mittee members and worked long hours taking
snapshots, developing the film, and laying out the
pages. When the book was finally brought in on
schedule, because of Joel's efforts more than anyone else's, his fellow workers did not even invite
him to the wrap party. Once again, he was the odd
man out.

"He was just devastated, absolutely devastated," said Jeanne. "He was almost single-handedly responsible for that book being out on time and they just dismissed him. He was always able to hide his pain in the past, but he couldn't hide the pain from that incident. He was heartbroken. And so was I."

Because of his array of learning disabilities, Joel's grades were average at best, which caused a rift with his father over what educational path he would take. "Dad wanted me to go to [a local] community [college]," said Joel. "He was like, 'we will knock out the basic credits you need as cheaply as possible, and after a year or two there you will go somewhere [else].' And he was firm on this. Every other kid is filling out applications [to] Brown [and] Stanford. They had these lists of colleges, and I had done no college research at all."

Joel dutifully, but miserably, went off to Nassau Community College, feeling as much like an outcast as he always had. If he had any illusions about reinventing himself in a new environment he soon realized that Nassau, located just a few miles from his home, was not the place to do it. "If you want to meet people and have a group of friends, community college is not the place to go," he explained. "The period ends and the parking lot empties. There is no college life at all."

Like so many of the other unfinished projects that would in many ways define him, Joel completed only one course at Nassau. That failure was only exacerbated by the forward strides his father made during the same period. Ben left his longtime employer to take a more prestigious, higher-paying position as a structural engineer at a national laboratory that was headquartered on Long Island.

With only one class to his credit at Nassau, Joel made plans to attend Brockport in the fall of 1978. Thinking that at Brockport he might finally be able to get himself out of the social slump he always seemed to be in, he became obsessed over the fact that he had no sexual experience. Because he presumed everyone else his age had experience, he was determined to get some before leaving for school. The last thing he wanted was to be known as the only virgin in the dormitory.

In the months prior to his departure he began patronizing prostitutes in Hempstead, a rundown town not far from his home. He wound up getting much more than he initially anticipated. For twenty dollars he could speak to any women he wanted, with no fear whatsoever of rejection. Before long he could not keep his mind off them. Because he always had such a difficult time with intimacy on any level, those brief encounters suited him fine. He now realizes it was nearly impossible for him to look anyone in the eye, much less experience their body on anything other than a primal level. By paying for sex, it was easy for him to view it with the same lack of emotion he would display when graduating to murder.

"The whole idea is it's [an] assembly line," he explained. "There's no foreplay, it's get it over with as fast as we can, push all the right buttons, get him out of here in two minutes flat. It almost becomes habitual." By the time Joel arrived at Brockport his desire for hookers would outweigh any academic aspirations.

From the geographical perspective of Long Island, which is located more than four hundred miles to the southeast, the village of Brockport is in the hinterlands. It sits in the midst of the snow belt, about twenty miles south of Lake Ontario. Separating the southeastern quadrant of the province of Ontario in east central Canada and northwest New York State, it is the smallest of the Great Lakes but mammoth by any other standard of measure. In the dead of winter the wind hurls itself off the lake and whips itself into a frenzy as it travels south along Route 19. By the time it reaches Brockport's Main Street, the tornado-like gusts can make the sleepy little village feel like the coldest place on earth. Because Brockport's winters traditionally start early and end late, it is not uncommon to trudge through several inches of snow after leaving a mid-October World Series party, or to have the joy of an eagerly anticipated spring break from sub-zero weather broken up by mid-to-late-April snowstorms.

While Brockport offers an array of undergraduate and graduate curricula, including theater, art, communication, anthropology, biological sciences, chemistry, African and Afro-American studies, earth sciences, and English, it has always been renowned for its physical education program more than anything else. Mockingly referred to as Jockport, it has graduated scores of student athletes with teaching degrees in physical education. Of equal renown are its twenty-three male and female Division III sports teams, which are known as the Golden Eagles. Over the years the school has produced hundreds of All-Conference, All-Region, All-State, and All-American players, as well as scores of individual national champions and dozens of academic All-Americans. A notable coach during our tenure there was Bill Van Gundy. Not only was he a collegiate coaching legend, but his son Jeff, who briefly attended Brockport in the late seventies, later established a lofty hoop legacy as the coach of the New York Knicks.

Even when an Owens-Corning plant on the outskirts of town employed hundreds of workers before closing down for good several decades ago, the college was the center of the universe in Brockport. Civic leaders and ordinary citizens alike are immensely proud of Brockport's designation as an all-American college town. With a non-student population of just 8,700 residents, and only about 2,500 families living in Brockport proper, it is as small and cozy a municipality as you will find anywhere. Some of that tranquility is disrupted when nearly 12,000 students converge on the town in early September and stay until June. While Brockport has never been besieged by anything remotely resembling a crime epidemic, like so many other college towns, the only recurrent problem seems to be weekend bar brawls between drunken students and local rowdies, who are derogatorily referred to as townies by the mostly out-of-town student body.

To this day, local residents and civic leaders bask in the glory of the week they hosted the fifth International Special Olympics in the summer of 1979. The community had long been an avid supporter of the Games, and Brockport even served as the site for the 1975 and 1976 state games. Thousands of residents helped out in any way they could, by volunteering their time to keep scores, run errands, do chores, prepare food, or serve as hosts and chaperones. Many even lent a spare room in their home free of charge to a visiting athlete or sponsor.

Brockport is also a desirable suburb of Rochester, a city of a quarter of a million that lies sixteen miles to the east. Although there is no shortage of urban blight and despair in Rochester, it is regularly deemed by pollsters to be one of the safest medium-sized cities in the nation. The bedrock of the community is the Eastman Kodak Company, which has employed thousands of fiercely loyal workers for over a century. The company is viewed with reverence by most of its workers, many of whom live in Brockport, which is about as far removed geographically from Long Island as it is philosophically.

"So I get to Brockport, and I'm a freshman flat out," said Joel. "Only I am nineteen, and everyone else is eighteen. And that started causing its own problems. By that time I was having problems with depression."

But Joel did make several significant inroads during his time there. He became a highly respected member of the photography club and even became serious enough with a girl to move in with her. But it did not take long for the bottom to fall out. "I was basically seriously depressed by that time," he recalls. "[Anti-depression and anxiety] medication probably would have helped me out in the world, but it wasn't around twenty years ago. The apartment looked like a tornado, and she got tired of living that way. I was sleeping [all the time], just not functioning. She said 'if you don't pass your subjects, if you don't get it together, I am going to rethink this whole relationship.' "

Joel had no idea how to engage in a healthy, mutually loving relationship. His girlfriend tried desperately to talk to him about it, but he was incapable of introspection. What the girlfriend did not know was that Joel was leading a clandestine life, one that regularly took him to Rochester to cavort with prostitutes. "Going out on the streets was my little secret world," he recounted. "That world never mixed with my normal, everyday world unless I needed money and had to steal from the regular world to pay a bill or if I was late for work. Generally no one knew that I was going out. It was just my little thing."

But his visits were taking a heavy toll on his personal relationship. His only experience was with hookers, so the assembly line process had become second nature to him. Not surprisingly, that did not sit well with his girlfriend, who was being introduced to her own sexuality by a clumsy, inhibited, and seemingly inconsiderate lover. Although unaware of his outside forays, she rightly believed he was making no effort to learn the basics of lovemaking, even though she was a caring, patient, and enthusiastic partner.

"I performed a little too fast," recalled Joel. "I didn't realize it at the time, [but patronizing prostitutes] became a problem [in my personal encounters]. She was in an amorous mood one night and she was looking for a night of romance and I was Mr. Automatic. She never spoke to me about it, I found out later on, but that basically ended our sex life. It ended the relationship pretty much, too."

What should have been a positive and exciting time for Joel was instead a period of great duress. Even his involvement in the photography club, where he was respected by everyone, brought no relief. "Artistic shooting was what motivated me," he said. "I was on the school paper for that reason, I had done the [high school] yearbook for that reason. What I was doing wasn't just an exercise in futility. I showed promise. I had professors, I had professionals tell me 'this one's pretty good, the rest of them you can chuck, but yeah, you have an eye here.' This is how you improve, and I would take the [necessary] classes. There was a photograph I took at Brockport [of] a guy sunbathing, leaning back on his skateboard. And the way the sweat and musculature was, it was a heck of a photo. I took it from above and there were all these little patterns around him. [But] I always underrated my skills. I [didn't] have that self-esteem to say, 'Yeah, I'm a good photographer.'"

It is easy for Joel to praise his work now, but he

certainly wasn't doing so then. Nor would he have been able to accept a compliment, even from a fellow student like me whom he had just met and who had no hidden agenda. It was not a feeling he was at all used to, much less comfortable with. To be accepted at any level by anybody, but especially a peer, completely confounded him. But such deep emotional terrain was not discussed by us that evening. In fact, Joel would never discuss those problems, or any other problems, until much later. Sadly for his seventeen victims and the countless family members and friends they left behind, the subject would not be broached until he was being interviewed by a battery of court-appointed psychiatrists, having already transformed himself into a skillful killer.

Because Joel rarely drank and never used drugs, he could find no way to socially interact with his fellow students while at Brockport. Nor could he find any athletic outlet. He had always been a self-described procrastinator and had recently been diagnosed with dyslexia. He did not excel in the academic arena either. Once again, Joel, an inveterate loner, found himself seeking impersonal comfort—this time in the company of prostitutes.

As Joel's passion for hookers increased, it required him to live his life under a veil of deceit. While he could always procure the services of a prostitute fairly easily, in every other facet of his life he was awkward, clumsy, and fumbling. "I never picked up anyone in a bar," said Joel. "If I ever attempted it I would break out in hives. They [prostitutes] held me back from everything, from a career and also a normal relationship."

One particularly awkward incident with his Brockport girlfriend still resonates with him, even though it is now more than twenty years after the fact. It is only in hindsight that Joel can realize how consuming his passion for prostitutes had become at the time. "We had gone to the mall and [found] one of these little antique fairs, where people set up little card tables and it is almost like a garage sale," he explained. "We were walking around, looking at some of the stuff, and there [was this] old photo of Teddy Roosevelt. I haggle the guy down to sixteen dollars. I bought it and didn't think nothing of it and she took it as 'we are low on money and we can't make the rent, how dare you spend sixteen bucks on this piece of garbage.'

"So we had a little argument over that. And I'm sitting there, having just got money sent up from mom and dad to pay the rent, but knowing I had blown thirty-five, forty bucks the previous weekend on one of my little wanderings. If she knew I blew fifty when she is banshee about sixteen, you know, whoa! It was pointed out to me that if we were going to do this [live together], we were going to have to pay bills [before anything else]. And I was oblivious."

Joel is quick to point to his own shortcomings as the reason his relationship failed with his college girlfriend, as did another relationship a few years later. Both showed much early promise. "[The college relationship] ended because I was [a] mental basket case at the time and she got tired," he recalled. "And the other one I gave up on because I saw it happening again. The first relationship, had these selective serotonin reuptake inhibitors [antidepressants] been around, which is the Paxil and Prozac family, [things might have been different]. I had been such a couch potato and a nonfunctioning person. [Had I not been so depressed] we probably would have gone on to have a relationship for the long term."

Although he loved the thrill associated with forbidden sex, Joel still entertained thoughts of eventually living what he perceived to be a normal life. When out on the streets—long before the killings began—he would often pass himself off as an overworked, underpaid, and beleaguered suburban husband and father, making it apparent that on some deep subconscious level he craved the sense of normality he knew he could never have. "That was part of the fantasy on the streets," he said. "I wanted to be normal, yeah. I don't think anybody wakes up and wants to be in Attica. You go through school, you pick a major, you hopefully meet somebody at school, and you want to have the normal picket fence and three kids and a dog and a cat and get on with life. Very few people start out saying 'Oh gee, my goal in life is to wind up in Attica.' I don't think anybody starts out that way."

As oblivious as Joel was of his own problems then, he was similarly oblivious of the health dangers associated with such a reckless lifestyle. With the AIDS crisis still several years away, unsafe sex was regularly practiced in back seats and on college campuses throughout the country. But Joel, never one to consider the ramifications of his behavior to begin with, was especially careless, even in an era that was practically defined by carefree, casual sex. "Over the Brockport time, [I would get] dime-sized and nickel-sized lesions that [were] incredibly painful," he recalled. "I used to get them in the back of my throat, couldn't swallow. I would be drooling for three days, banked [a] hundred-four-degree temperature. Eventually I found a doctor in Brockport who, instead of saying it's not treatable, which the virus isn't, he treated the infection with penicillin and Tylenol with codeine. So, I'd be asleep for three days, basically."

Stressed out over his inability to assimilate smoothly, Joel said he experienced several of these attacks at school. "Just the whole stretch at Brockport brought it on," he said. "The last time I had an attack was prior to my arrest. I haven't had one since I've been locked up, but I've had other herpes [attacks] since I've been locked up."

While Joel failed to gain much from his time at college, Brockport came to represent something completely different for me. Before I enrolled, in September 1977, I spent nearly three years traversing the country hoping to find myself in the most unlikely places. I scraped rust off barges in Florida, installed sewers in new housing tracts in Houston, mined for ore in New Mexico, and lived in a junkie-infested flophouse a block from the water in the Ocean Beach section of San Diego. I had gone off on a whirlwind journey in search of myself, but somehow got derailed along the way. After years of living recklessly, I enrolled in Brockport at age twenty, more confused than ever.

During the Special Olympics, which took place three months before I met Joel, I finally began to get serious about my studies and developed a zeal for writing against deadline. While working for a daily school newspaper called *The Olympics Special: The Official Newspaper of the International Summer Special Olympics*, I spent the week following around such celebrities as Muhammad Ali, Ted Kennedy, and Arnold Schwarzenegger, as well as seeking out human interest stories on my own. I was responsible for filing at least two stories per day, and the energy and enthusiasm I will forever associate with that week were unforgettable. Not only did I emerge with a wealth of practical experience that I was certain would suit me well in the workforce one day, the way the entire town opened their arms and their hearts to the most humble, noble, and determined of athletes was tremendously heartwarming and uplifting.

I came to believe that Norman Rockwell's vision of America really did exist, and that one did not have to look further than Brockport USA to see it. Even though I left town in December 1980, armed with a degree in journalism and the wide-eyed wonderment of youth, in many subtle ways my heart still belongs there. I finally got a glimmer of what I wanted out of life, as well as some of the tools to go after it. For that, I will be forever grateful.

On the official Brockport web site recently, the school boasted that it had produced no shortage of "Nurses, CPAs, Police Officers, Journalists, Psychologists, Oceanographers." Having become both a successful international boxing journalist and a New York City police detective since leaving Brockport two decades earlier, I felt a slight twinge of pride at being part of the school's considerable legacy. Like Joel, I always had a difficult time with inclusion, especially when it had to do with such a large organization. But nowhere on the web page did it make mention of its most famous and notorious alumnus, Joel Rifkin, the most savage serial killer in New York State history.

I HAD ONLY SEEN JOEL ONCE AFTER THE fight, when he dropped off action photos of the bout and its even more action-packed aftermath. The quality of his work left little doubt that he could have made it as a professional shooter. I always believed that, as socially awkward as he was, he would immerse himself in his photography and carve out a rewarding career. But Joel dropped out of Brockport not long after we met, and I would not see him again until the Attica visit two decades later.

Joel had no way of knowing that I had attached an inexplicable association to him. Just ten weeks after the Rochester riots I realized just how much of a positive impression he had left on me. While in John Griffin's training camp, I was surprised at what a rush I got out of boxing. I was initially shocked at my ability to bloody the noses of more experienced opponents, but I was also glad to have finally found an acceptable way to unleash my aggressions. It was not something I was always very comfortable with. As a second or third grader I used to incessantly bully a neighborhood boy by knocking his books to the ground, then mockingly repeating his father's name. After making him cry, I would be overcome by guilt and shame.

Around the same time I also had a pet hamster. One day I put her in a cardboard paper towel roll, aimed for a bed, and blew as hard as I could. She landed on her side, relatively unharmed, but dazed and frightened. I still chastise myself for committing that lone act of animal cruelty, as well as for the actions toward the victim of my bullying. Fortunately, those actions taught me that I had too much of a conscience to be mean, and I began equating my "power" with negative feelings. As a result I regularly harnessed my aggressive tendencies throughout my childhood for fear of being hurtful. Boxing finally afforded me a healthy alternative.

On the night of Griffin's bout, which he would lose by a second-round knockout, a local heavyweight and big ticket seller named Dick Embleton was scheduled to fight, but his opponent failed to show. With the promoters frantically looking for a replacement, I pleaded with Griffin's trainer and manager, a former heavyweight title challenger named Dave "Ziggy" Zyglewicz, to let me fill the void. As I sat in the dressing room preparing to embark on a professional boxing career, I kept thinking of Joel doing something equally unimaginable, like jumping out of airplanes in order to fill his portfolio with photos of parachutists drifting in the wind.

After I won what the local newspaper called a "wild first round," Embleton connected with a Hail-Mary left hook that shattered my nose and sent me to the canvas face first in the second round. I managed to get to my feet by the count of five, but the referee wisely called a halt to my inauspicious ring debut. Although I had lost the battle, I felt I had won the war. Overwhelmed by a newfound feeling of physical prowess, I fought several more times over the next four years, losing more than I won but grateful for the experience.

Sharing a dressing room with me that night was a cocky and loquacious young fighter named Charley Newell. He was a minimum security inmate at a nearby correctional facility who had been let out on a work-release program to box. Two fights after mine he squared off against Marlon Starling, a Hartford product who would become the welterweight champion of the world a few years later. Starling was en route to a boring decision win over Newell when the crowd screaming for more action. The boos soon turn to chants and finally, in the seventh round, Starling began hitting Newell with an array of vicious punches. After a final, crushing blow, an ominous hush engulfed the arena as Newell's head hit the canvas with a sickening thud. He was carried into the dressing room on a stretcher, his eyelids closed but twitching, spittle gurgling in the corners of his mouth, and a thin, grayish substance leaking from his ears. Embleton and I stood over his body as doctors tried to revive him, but Newell died two days later. While he took with him my own sense of invincibility, his death also left me with an urgency to live life to its fullest.

What I found most bewildering was Starling's reaction to the tragedy. It still mystifies me as much as Joel's reaction to his own killings. He did a victory jig and reveled in the accolades of the fans. From my vantage point, neither Starling nor Joel seemed to be the least bit concerned about their role in the death of fellow human beings. While part of me loathed them for their callousness, I could not help being secretly envious of their ability to live so free of guilt and shame. Because I had been controlled by a disproportionate amount of those emotions for all of my life, being devoid of them seemed like such a luxury to me. That, I believe, was the origin of my fascination with criminals. It had nothing to do with getting a vicarious thrill from their actions, or even a latent desire to mimic them. It was as if they had the ultimate freedom of all: living without any sense of responsibility or accountability.

By the time I fought Embleton, Joel had already dropped out of Brockport and my perception of him as a world-class photographer was as far from reality as possible. His relationship over and his grades dismal, Joel had returned home more adrift than he'd ever been. He remembers this as one of the most painful periods of his life. "I had just broken up with [my girlfriend], and it's career time," he recalled. "So I joined up with the parent company of Record World, worked in the warehouse for a little over a year. Then I went into the management training program. They didn't promote me [on their own], I asked for it. The idea was simple: go from assistant manager to manager, maybe to district supervisor, maybe transfer to another company. But I liked retail, [I wanted] to stay in the retail field, work as a store manager, junior executive, whatever. The only thing that got in the way was doing the paperwork. A simple little daily report I couldn't handle."

Suddenly Joel found himself regressing back into childhood, and his frustration, self-loathing, and self-doubt mounted. "I had supervisors come in and work with me, I had extra sessions with managers, I had sessions with my father," he recalled. "I just could not get the accounting skills to do the paperwork."

Even though his job brought him so much anxiety, Joel was determined not to lose it. Discussing that period of his life seems as painful to him as recalling the childhood horrors that he suffered through. Oddly enough he seems perfectly sane talking about murder and dismemberment, but downright unstable when discussing his tenure at Record World. Besides being overwhelmed by his many responsibilities, Joel was unable to be on time. As a result, his supervisors were forced to keep tabs on him, even though he was in a management training program.

"Some mornings I came in early," he recalled. "It was weird, you really couldn't be late, but [the manager] always knew if I was in the store later than I was supposed to be. As long as the store opened at nine o'clock and I was there, you're on time. But [the manager] wanted you there at 8:30, so my [store] phone would be ringing at 8:32. I had to run through the store to get to the phone [and say] 'I'm here.'"

But for Joel, the most intense terror was associated with closing up the store at night. "There are a few nights I remember that very bad feeling when they're turning off the lights and we were in the exact middle of the circuit board," he explained. "So [the lights] would race at you from the two sides and at a point [there] was total darkness. And I'd be sitting there with the bank deposit bag and the safe open, watching the lights race toward me, throwing everything in the safe, kicking it, spinning it, then running through the store with the lights out because I was that late trying to do the bags."

Although it's likely that Joel would eventually have been dismissed for his incompetence, it was actually his dishonesty that got him fired. "You're allowed as an employee to get an employee discount," he explained. "It was the Christmas season. I was buying albums for a friend and he picked out the albums. He went in the store, made sure it was in stock, told me to get this, this, and this. And they knew and they fired me for abuse of my employee discount. But when I tried to get an employee fired for that I couldn't do it because the union got in the way."

Weeks earlier, Joel had caught an employee red-handed, stealing merchandise, but instead of being praised for taking swift and decisive action he was humiliated by his superiors. "I had a guy ringing up albums that he wasn't even clever about," he said laughingly. "I looked at the [register] tape because he had a check come on right behind it, and it was like since when do we sell albums for fifty cents? He was so obvious. So I wrote him up and this was like his second or third write-up and he was gone. The next day a guy walks in with an attaché case, [from the] union. It came down to he was prohibited from working the register, but he could still be employed by the company and work on the floor. And we're talking an eighteen-year-old kid had more power than I had. That was the first real hard failure. I was getting physically ill. I was having angina attacks."

As Joel was trying to establish a foothold at Record World, I was living in New York trying to establish a career as a writer. Having been selected for an internship at *The New York Times* during my last semester at Brockport, I foolishly assumed I would have no trouble landing a reporting job with a major newspaper. I even declined several job offers from small newspapers around the country. Three years later, while floundering around New York with dismal career prospects, I joined the police department. It had nothing to do with any degree of altruism or sense of civic responsibility. If I had to work for a living, I figured it would be best to do so in a somewhat unconventional fashion. By doing something not everyone would be willing to do, I convinced myself I wasn't selling out.

After graduating from the police academy in

June 1983, I was sent for six months of field training to the Washington Heights section of Manhattan, which was about to become ground zero for
the crack cocaine epidemic. I was then transferred
to the South Bronx, where I was assigned to the
midnight shift with my partner, Michael Whyte.
After logging hundreds of felony arrests without
receiving one civilian complaint for brutality or
discourtesy, we shared Cop of the Year honors in
1985. On the night we received the coveted
plaque from a grateful Community Council and a
City Council Citation from a local politician, I remembered the night Whyte and I came face to
face with a deranged man who had just fired two
rounds into a crowd of youngsters on a street that
ran through the heart of a public housing development. Minutes after starting our midnight shift, in
full uniform and in a marked department auto, we
heard shots and saw two muzzle flashes as the
screaming, panicked crowd dispersed wildly from
the shooting area. We did what cops everywhere
do on a daily basis: raced to the scene as everyone
else raced away.

The gunman, a black man in his late thirties,
never left our field of vision. As we screeched to a
halt and exited the vehicle, our guns extended forward in a combat stance, we ordered him to drop
the weapon. He stared at us through feral eyes,
the revolver firmly in his grasp and pointing in our

direction. Why we did not take him out I still don't know. After all, he made no attempt to drop the gun or flee when he saw us coming. It certainly would have been reasonable to conclude that he was about to engage us in a firefight.

"Drop the gun," we shouted in unison, as forcefully as possible. Part of me said shoot, while a more powerful voice told me not to. As we repeated the order to drop the gun, six, seven, possibly eight times, the man just continued to fix a steely glare on us. The crowd began to gather around us again, and while intently watching our every move, they grew braver and more raucous by the second. Little did it matter that they were all black, as was the gunman, and would probably have called it a public execution had we fired. All they knew was that they wanted revenge for being fired upon, and they wanted us to be the avengers. "Smoke the motherfucker," someone yelled as the situation picked up momentum with each spine-tingling second. "Cap him," railed another. "Kill him," were the last words we heard before charging and disarming the gunman in one fleeting moment of sheer terror.

After we slammed him up against his own car and retrieved the still-loaded gun, Whyte ran around to the passenger's side, where another man sat. On the open door of the glove box sat a small bottle of liquor and two Dixie cups that were half full. The two men, we later learned, had been sitting in their car, drinking peacefully, when they were chided by a group of teenagers. Whyte ordered the obviously intoxicated passenger out of the auto. While I was preoccupied with safeguarding the gunman, the adrenaline still pumping through me like an electric current, Whyte forcefully pulled the passenger out of the vehicle and attempted to stand him up against the car. Only when the man dropped straight down and landed with a thud, still in a vertical position, did we realize that, along with being both unarmed and harmless, he was also legless.

While we were processing the arrest at the precinct, the gunman's daughter came by and ardently thanked us for not opening fire. She explained that he was a brain-damaged Vietnam veteran who had spent time in a prisoner of war camp and was regularly taunted by neighborhood youngsters because of his oddball behavior. Until I learned what had become of Joel, this was the most powerful lesson I had had about the fact that things are rarely what they seem at first glance. Not when it comes to police work, and certainly not when it comes to serial killers.

Unlike Joel, I never toyed with the idea of killing someone; not for revenge, not for pleasure, not even in a combat situation where I had every right to do so. To this day, I commend myself more for not shooting that man than for anything else in my police career. I have no doubt that he had no intention of harming either me or Officer Whyte, and I now believe he was hoping *we* would kill him. Since that night, a new phenomenon called "suicide by cop" has made its way into the lexicon of American culture. Although I will never be sure, I believe that was his sole motivation on that memorable evening.

Once the adventure of being a street cop wore off, I felt like a civil service sellout as I imagined Joel on assignment in exotic, faraway locales shooting for *National Geographic* and *Life* magazines. I also became acutely aware of the sometimes precarious, indistinguishable line between lawbreakers and lawmen. The fact that Joel and I had many similar experiences and wound up on the opposite ends of the societal spectrum still intrigues me. Like some of Joel's conflicting behavioral patterns, some of my actions were difficult to explain.

Once I transferred to the plainclothes narcotics division in 1986, I was always eager to be the first one through the door while executing a dangerous search warrant. Yet I had never been caught up in the macho cop culture where I felt a need to prove myself to others. Although I had no shortage of good friends on the job, we rarely, if ever, exchanged our war stories while socializing. Putting myself into these dangerous situations had nothing to do with gallantry. Nor was it about trying to impress others with my sense of nobility. I guess, like Joel's killings, my bravado was the only way I knew to feel truly alive.

5

THROUGHOUT THE EARLY TO MID EIGHT-
ies, Joel, who was now in his late twenties, was perpetually unemployed and constantly at odds with
his father, who was diagnosed with prostate cancer
in the middle of the decade. What little money Joel
was able to sporadically scrape together doing odd
jobs was spent on his regular forays into the streets.
He also worked occasionally on an autobiographi-
cal screenplay called "The Frosh," which chronicled his days as a freshman at Brockport. It was
while immersed in that project that he met a
woman with whom he initially hoped to have a
somewhat normal relationship.

Joel says he met Kathleen Dever* on the East

*Pseudonym.

12th Street stroll, while she, perhaps trying to conceal her life as a prostitute, told the police that they met in a Queens pizzeria where she was working as a waitress. He passed himself off as a New York University student who had just completed a screenplay. Dever, who was about a decade older than Joel, fancied herself a writer and claimed she hired him to assist in a screenplay she was working on.

Joel soon moved into the squalid West 49th Street apartment she was already sharing with another person. While at first Joel thought he might have a meaningful relationship with the tanned, seemingly healthy blond woman, their relationship quickly deteriorated. "I spent about a month, month and a half there," he recalled. "The guy who had it, his father had passed away, and he moved in and didn't tell the landlord. I don't know if he was paying rent on it or not. The place was a general mess, the plumbing was always overflowing."

According to Joel things got progressively worse when Dever, whom he described as a prostitute and heavy drug user, became consumed by paranoia. "I don't know if it was a real event or cocaine paranoia, but she thought that there was a dealer on the streets that was trying to kill her," he recalled. "And I had to help her move, so I showed up one day with a car that I had borrowed and moved her from this one squat to another squat. And then she wanted to know if I could hang out and follow her on her strolls, in case this guy showed up [so] I could at least scare him off by being a witness."

Because Joel rarely "dated" any women other than prostitutes, one has to wonder if he was angry that they were the only women he could get. One might also question Joel's motivation for a somewhat normal relationship, especially in light of its timing. In his father's eyes, Joel had always been a failure in relationships, as well as in his educational and vocational pursuits. Could this have been a subconscious attempt to gain respect from his ailing father? Or was he genuinely interested in having a conventional relationship, even if it was with an unconventional woman? Could he have been taken in by the fact that she claimed to be a writer and on the fast track to success? Could he have been lured by her grandiosity?

Joel was both repelled and fascinated by Dever's street instincts, and watched in awe as she went about her daily business. In his mind she epitomized junkie chic. "She had a book of regulars [and] she would almost beg some of them, not so much for a date, but 'would they cruise by the lobby of my building and drop a twenty on me?' She had a ritual. She had to get a new pair of cheap stockings every time she went out, [as well as] a pint of Southern Comfort or Jack Daniel's. Like she had to get drunk to go out. She went out to the streets because of her cocaine addiction."

Although they had sex on only one occasion—right after their initial meeting—and Dever's life was in as much chaos as Joel's, he developed a strong crush on her. Joel now believes it had more to do more with the element of danger than anything else. Whatever his motivations were, Joel's attempts at a real-life romance were foiled once again. Things came to a halt for good after she stole a camera and a good deal of cash from him.

"[She] was a total con [wo]man and eventually ripped me off big time, stole a camera, stole over two grand," Joel recalled. "The camera I loaned her like an idiot, and she claimed it was stolen on the street. And one night I was gonna try and find a place in the city to crash, so I basically got hold of over two grand. She had to pay off a debt, and she was in the con where she was gonna get out of town and go someplace else. And she did it real sweet, where I thought I had lost it, but she had lifted it [from my boot]."

When Dever's photo was found in Joel's room after his arrest, investigators were certain she was another yet-to-be-identified victim. After a mad scramble to ascertain her identity, she was tracked to a motel in Toms River, New Jersey. She told police that she was HIV-positive and that, although she and Joel only had a brief business relationship, she had also met his mother. She said she fired him as her writing assistant because, "He wasn't doing anything, he was just sitting around. I couldn't stand to be around him."

By that point in his life, Joel had pretty much given up on any of his earlier dreams. Making matters worse for him was having to watch as his handful of childhood East Meadow friends moved on with their own lives, while he remained the outsider. Many of Joel's most normal and happy memories are of the times he spent playing weekly games of pinochle and bridge with those friends, right up until shortly before his arrest. Although he often compared himself unfavorably to them, they were the closest thing to family, or anything conventionally positive, in his life. Amazingly, Joel was able to walk on a high wire between both worlds without ever falling off. Even before he started killing, he never shared stories with them about his nocturnal wanderings into the city's underbelly, which often occurred right after their games. They would be as shocked as everyone else when it was later discovered that he was such a nefarious killer. "Some of the killings were after the card games," said Joel. "Some of the dating was after the card games." Strangely, he could not remember if he had lost money during any of those pre-murder games, which might have contributed to his negative mindset at the time.

"One by one they were starting to get married off, [which I guess is] the natural events [of things]," he lamented. "I went to two of these weddings and I got stress illness at both of them. Not so bad [at] the first one, [but at] the second one, [I was] feverish. I don't know if it was just losing a friend, or [the fact] it wouldn't be happening to me. I was put at a table with other singles. I couldn't move that day. I [had] a hundred three fever."

Joel now believes that medication might have brought him out of his shell, but being such a loner, he couldn't bear the thought of seeking professional help. His parents had brought him to a psychiatrist as a teenager, a memory he still finds troubling. "It's really hard to accept that you have a mental problem," he said. "It's like, no, I don't have a problem. I'm just fine, I'm normal. A lot of the social anxiety disorder is not wanting to go to a psychiatrist either, because you just relate to him as another stranger. If you can't relate in the sessions, the sessions aren't doing anything."

With his father's illness getting worse by the day, Joel began to feel more and more like a disappointment in his eyes. While living with Dever during the earlier stages of his father's illness, Joel would come home one night a week to lend moral support to his parents. "At that time Thursday night had a really intense TV lineup and him and my mom would like to watch it from almost eight o'clock to eleven o'clock," he recalled. "So I would join them and spend the night with them, just to be with him, trying to be close. Unfortunately, as his illness progressed I'd give him a hug goodbye, [but] he wouldn't hug back, his arms would just stay limp."

The family learned that Ben was terminally ill in 1986. As upset as Joel was over the prospect of losing his father, part of him was anxious to get one last shot at vindication. Ben, who by that time had an experimental chemotherapy pump affixed to his belt through which medication flowed throughout the day, persuaded Joel, then twenty-eight, to take one class at the nearby State University of New York at Farmingdale. He promised him that if he earned a B or better, he would pay for a full-time curriculum the following semester. Joel, who truly wanted his father to see him as something other than an aimless and shiftless failure before he died, eagerly and enthusiastically accepted the challenge.

"He wanted me to have a college education," explained Joel, who moved back home once his brief relationship with Dever was over. "I tried and failed, tried again, failed, tried again, failed. I'm making one more shot at it, one more try. I picked biology because biology was hard, but it wasn't as hard as math. We wanted a true test. I couldn't take reading or writing. I couldn't take art. It had to be a true test. This was the agreement and I'm working like a fiend. I'm really stressing out and concentrating."

Just before the midterm exam Ben took a lethal combination of barbiturates, fell into a coma, and died three days later. Joel still blames himself for his father's desperate action. "I don't know if he thought I was gonna fail and he didn't want to face another failure, because the timing was so close," said Joel. "Maybe I drove him to an early suicide because he didn't want to see me fail again. But at the same time I was incredibly angry at the timing. That was my shot."

Joel said he took the test on "automatic pilot," and received his grade, a 90, on the day before his father's death. "The doctor said 'we think people can hear in a coma, so why don't you tell him how you did,'" he recalled. "I said 'Gee, Dad, I got a ninety, isn't that great?' I [still] don't know if I drove him to an early death or if he was just tired [of all the suffering]."

Joel's stirring eulogy at his father's service began with the words, "My father didn't give me life, but he gave me love." Those words, as well as the supportive feelings his family conveyed to each other throughout this difficult time, brought Joel some much-needed comfort. But other more pervasive feelings were working hard to counteract it. Knowing how proud his father always wanted to be of his only son and what a bitter disappointment he had actually become caused Joel incredible heartache. Many emotional issues were left in tatters by his father's death and Joel spiraled into an emotional abyss.

Years later many psychological experts would point to this episode as ample proof of Joel's psychopathic tendencies. They were critical of the fact that the only way he could view his father's death was as an event that ruined his own chance at redemption. It was as if he was angry with his dad for taking himself out of his own misery and denying his son a well-deserved pat on the back. The second half of the following comment by Joel only seems to strengthen the arguments of his critics. "This is one of the least understood things, where I have been said to be very self-centered or very narcissistic and all these other fancy words," he explained. "If I succeeded with this [getting a good final grade], I would have got a hug. It would have been a meaningful hug."

Falling into the deepest depression of his life, Joel sought even more comfort than usual from the prostitutes he had now been frequenting for a decade. Even an embarrassing arrest for solicitation in August 1987 in Hempstead, Long Island, did not thwart him. Joel, who had asked an under-cover police officer for sex, was eventually ordered to pay a nominal fine. All the arrest did was force him to be more careful and vigilant in the future. He would avoid a second arrest by never again being the first to speak the incriminating words while looking to engage a hooker on the street. By this time Joel's proclivity for prostitutes had evolved into a full-blown compulsion. He had become a man possessed.

6

FOR THE NEXT TWO YEARS, JOEL'S FEEL-

ings of worthlessness greatly intensified. He visited prostitutes with increasing frequency, always
spending more money than he made and always
mired in debt. He viewed the city as his great escape and loved the anonymity of the streets. To
him the city represented a lawless playground
where anything could be had for a price, where he
could be anybody he wanted to be, where any type
of transgression would go unnoticed. He sup-
ported his habit by working a series of odd jobs,
most of which were related to landscaping.

"I couldn't put two nickels together," he recalled. "I took a paycheck and if I didn't pre-spend
it, it would be gone by Monday. The whole focus
of my life was the streets. It wasn't a positive

thing. It was a negative thing. To me, it was a beast. I would get paid on a Friday, and have to borrow gas money from somebody on Monday."

Joel went so far as to unfavorably compare his binging on women to the way the women he frequented binged on drugs. "If the girl had one thousand dollars' [worth of drugs], she could smoke one thousand dollars," he explained. "If I went into the city with one thousand dollars, I would go home with a tank of gas. If I went in with fifty dollars, the same with the girl, she could smoke fifty dollars and feel comfortable, where I could burn the fifty dollars and feel comfortable."

As streetwise as Joel believed himself to be, he was actually putty in a cunning streetwalker's hand. Even if he hid his money in different parts of his clothing or vehicle, more often than not they would find it. He gave up counting how many times he fronted women money for drugs, only to watch them disappear into the night. "I was ripped off at least a dozen times by different girls," he said. "Once was [when] I picked the girl up [and] we went to the Hempstead Motel [on Long Island]. She delays it. We end up undressing. She's just starting on her underwear. A knock at the door, the door comes flying open. It's her 'boyfriend.' [He says] 'I told you, never do this again,' yada, yada, yada. He grabs her clothes, grabs her, pulls her out of the room." Once he noticed that his money was missing, Joel realized he had been had in more ways than one. "It was a timing thing," he said. "Now I understand why the delay in getting undressed and getting the whole thing done.

"Then there was another girl, on Atlantic Avenue [in Brooklyn]," he continued. "Most of the girls have a favorite spot where they feel safe. So she's directing me to this grocery store parking lot. We pull in, drive up to the wall. Now the front of the car is facing the wall. This car pulls in behind me. Two guys get out and they do the cop routine. I never saw any badges, but they're claiming they're cops and they're claiming that she says you stole fifty dollars from her. I got only thirty dollars on me, so I gave them thirty and they drove off. And I pulled the other thirty I had underneath the seat and went back to the stroll and picked someone else up. There's all kinds of cons. It was amazing."

For all of the time he spent as a member of the urban nether world, Joel never got savvy to the rules of the street. Generally, his forays brought him more stress than relief. And he claims this was something he needed, not something he wanted. As much as he hated being controlled by such a perilous and degrading addiction, even after being robbed on numerous occasions, he was unable to stop. "The same girl ripped me off twice.

I fell for the same play twice," he said. "[She told me] 'I live with my grandmother, let me go see if she's awake and if I can sneak you into the house.' Both times [six months apart] she disappeared into the house and through the backyard. I don't even know if she lived in that house."

But in the end, it was Joel who used his meek appearance and frazzled, harmless demeanor to pull off the ultimate con of all. His reign of terror began in March 1989, two years to the month after his father's death. He had moved back in with his mother, who at the time was white-water rafting in Colorado. His sister was living away from home. On the night of his inaugural killing, things started out in typical fashion for him. Joel left Long Island around ten o'clock after watching an episode of *Kojak* on television.

He headed into the city, as he had hundreds of times before, and murderous thoughts were dancing around in his head. He had no reason to think that this would be the night he would finally cross the line from fantasy into reality. He often thought about bringing prostitutes back home but rarely had the chance. But this night was different. Still, he insists to this day that getting his first victim in the house was in no way part of a grander scheme to lure her to some private killing ground. Because he was perpetually nervous, easily spooked, and terrified of altering his life in any way, the thought of engaging in such a dangerous action was inconceivable to him. After all, by that time he estimates he had been with well over three hundred hookers, all of whom had been paid in full and left unharmed.

"That [strangulation fantasy] was used to sometimes jazz the evening up just on a mental level," he said. "I'd been with a long string of streetwalkers, so there were even fantasy games just to perk that up because even that got to be routine."

He first saw victim number one, a blond, emaciated, jewelry-adorned white girl with a Parkinson's-like tremor, on the First and Second Avenues stroll, between 11th and 12th Streets in Manhattan's East Village. She said her name was Susie. After they negotiated a price for her to accompany him to Long Island, the relationship quickly deteriorated and his blood began to boil. Before leaving the city she wanted to make a few stops for drugs. "First we stopped at her girlfriend's house," recalled Joel contemptuously. "Because you always have to take care of their narcotic need, their money need, and then they'll get around to taking care of your need.

"This girl had advanced HIV, she would shoot up and pass out," he added. "She's in this girl's bathroom for like hours." As she chatted and smoked with her friend for what seemed like an eternity, totally oblivious of her client, Joel became more and more upset. Once they left the friend's apartment, they arrived in East Meadow within a half hour. While it would have been obvious to anyone that Susie was completely out of her element in a world of manicured lawns and suburban serenity, Joel did not care. Because it was so late at night, he figured no one would see her enter the house, and he would just sneak her out in the morning. Joel's neighbors knew him as a bit of an eccentric nocturnal creature anyway. It was not unusual for him to come and go at all hours, nor was it unusual for him to work on jacked-up cars in front of his house into the wee hours of the morning.

Within minutes of entering the same home Joel and his sister grew up in, the two had sex—sex that was a prelude to murder. "[My fantasies] were a little more intense than regular," recalled Joel.

Afterward, he says, "she wanted to catch up on some sleep, I watched some MTV. She had something to eat. You know, casual hanging out." It did not take long for Susie to want more drugs. "She wanted to go out and get high again," said Joel, who was angered by the fact that his needs were being put second to Susie's desire for more drugs. "I agreed to drive her around [to] see if we could find something"

By this point Joel was not only outraged at Susie's single-mindedness, but he was also concerned about shopping for drugs on Long Island. While he had no compunctions about buying drugs for the girls in the city, he did not feel comfortable doing it so close to home. Looking back, Joel says he is still shocked at what happened next. In an instant, without warning, he transformed himself from a perpetual victim into a stone-cold killer. "I decided not to find my keys," he recalled blandly. "[I] found this thing, hit her with it, and that was the first time."

The "thing" was a howitzer shell he had recently bought at a military flea market. It weighed about ten or twelve pounds, and Joel estimated it was eighteen inches long and six to eight inches in diameter. "[I was hitting her] two-handed, like a baseball bat," he said. "Sideways, up from the top, all different ways. I just lost control. I stopped when I got tired."

Only after he was finished and sure she was dead did he begin to panic. "I remember running around, trying to turn the TV volume up, pulling the shades down," he said laughingly, as if recalling some spirited college high jinks. "I imagined the cops coming right to the doorway. [I was thinking] they can read minds, they know what happened." To his horror, Susie suddenly popped up on the couch in a last-ditch effort to salvage her life. She tore into her assailant, an out-of-shape but awkwardly strong one-hundred-seventy-pound man, with all the strength she could muster. "She bit my finger, almost to the bone," said Joel. "Eventually I pinned her against something and she died. I'm not sure if it was strangulation or smothering."

As he sopped up the blood and cleaned up the mess in the living room of the home where he had always found refuge from his tormentors, Joel did not realize that, in essence, he had died along with Susie on that cold, damp March morning. Not only did all of his aspirations, no matter how far-fetched or ill conceived, go up in smoke, but so did whatever remnants were left of his humanity. He would now have to live with a dirty little secret, one that excited him as much as it terrified him, and would eventually come to control him. It would take eighteen months for him to take another life, but when he did there would be no stopping him. He had finally found something he could do with conviction and expertise. Unfortunately, it was not something of which his father would have been proud.

WHILE THE INITIAL PANIC AND PARANOIA
Joel experienced over his first killing resurfaced regularly over the next eighteen months, he had no trouble falling asleep less than an hour after snuffing out the life of his first victim. He awoke a few hours later, then went about the business of disposing of her small body. His greatest fear came not from his newfound ability to kill with impunity, but over his belief that he would never get away with it. After all, he mused, he had never done anything well before. He managed to stuff Susie's body into a large plastic bag, then dragged it, bouncing with a thud on each step, into the basement. Asked if he realized at that moment that his life had been altered forever or if he ever questioned what had become of his existence, Joel was circumspect.

"It was one of the things that would circle around, and I would just shut it down," he explained. "I was more shocked by it. [I would tell myself] I really don't want to think about this and distract myself. [It was like] okay, it happened, it's never gonna happen again. If I make it go away I can pretty much, you know, pretend it didn't happen and go about a normal life. Then, of all things, there was a *Donahue* episode that summed it up. They were talking about the [Connecticut] wood chipper murder [where an airline pilot murdered his wife, then disposed of her body by shredding it in a wood chipper]. There was the usual panel of social workers and psychiatrists. And someone said, 'well, after the spirit leaves the body, it is just a body.'"

Having already compartmentalized his horrific actions, Joel found dismembering Susie's body as easy as killing her. "I reduced it to biology class," he explained in a disturbingly rational way, seemingly oblivious of the irony that he had recently excelled in a college level biology class taken at his dying father's behest. "It was just a straight dissection, done as fast as you can. Eventually I went with the idea of a scalpel, which I imitated with an X-Acto knife, and made very small, controlled cuts over the joints and popped the bones out of the sockets. As a kid you learn how to carve a turkey. You just go to the bone on the wing and the bone on the leg. You can't cut the bone with a knife, you find it and pop it."

As I listened to Joel ramble on in an emotionless drone, I had to keep reminding myself that, by virtue of being a journalist, I was not allowed the luxury of being judgmental. But even the most seasoned reporter would have had difficulty remaining impassive. The absolute calm in Joel's voice, coupled with his stolid demeanor, made my skin crawl. It was obvious that he felt no remorse, nor did he have any apparent interest in relegating these murderous memories to the furthermost environs of his mind. Sensing nothing awry in my bearing, Joel continued on without missing a beat.

He plucked out Susie's teeth with a pair of pliers, forced her head into an empty paint can, then stuffed different parts of her body into separate thirty-three-gallon garbage bags. He hauled the packages outside to his Ford F-350 pickup, and hurled them like weekend yard debris into the bed of the truck. He drove a few hours into New Jersey where he discarded the paint can in what he thought was a remote wooded area, then used all of his strength to throw the bag containing the legs into the woods at another nearby location. Driving back into New York City, he headed straight for an area near the East River in lower Manhattan, the same area where he had been serviced by streetwalkers countless times before. His head was spinning as he parked the truck and flung the bags containing Susie's arms and torso into the frigid, swirling waters.

The dank, dirty streets of the Lower East Side had become like a second home to him, perhaps even more of a refuge than his real home. He had grown so accustomed to going there, it was the only place where he felt completely comfortable. On Long Island he had to worry about such mundane things as disturbing his mother's perfectly manicured gardens or cleaning up after himself or not frazzling his sister's nerves when she was home for a visit. But out here he let his alter ego take over. He was the man in control, a discerning customer who got to choose which hooker he wanted and ultimately, as time wore on, whether she lived or died. It was a power he grew to relish.

The day after the murder Joel acknowledged to himself that he had done something wrong, but developed a method of disavowing any personal responsibility. "It is like a kid that breaks something that his mother has, a vase of flowers or something, and he just throws it out and pretends Mom will never notice," he rationalized. "And then Mom says, 'Hey, where's that picture frame?' 'I don't know, I haven't seen it in weeks.' Kids do these things. And I reacted the same way. I scrubbed everything. I cleaned everything, even stuff that wasn't even related. I pretended it never happened."

Less than one week later Joel heard on a local news radio station that Susie's head had been found by golfers near the seventh hole of a Hopewell, New Jersey, course. It rolled there after a rain storm, setting off a mammoth investigation. "I panicked, [had] a major anxiety attack," he said. "The whole thing kept repeating in my head. From the time I picked her up, it kept up like a continuous loop tape. It was almost an obsessive type of thinking."

Oddly enough, once his mother returned from her trip Joel did not feel the least bit awkward around her. "I had covered up for years, just going to the streets," he said. "From not only Mom, Dad, [but also my] sister [and] girlfriends. I pretty much lived with secrets [for my entire life]."

Even after her son committed his first murder, Jeanne Rifkin never detected anything unusual in his consistently oddball behavior. She had become so used to his eccentricities that nothing, no matter how awkward or bewildering, seemed out of the ordinary anymore. Although Joel was anxious over the discovery of Susie's head, he recovered from his initial panic and was able to behave normally around his mother. Despite residing under the same roof, the two of them had actually been living in separate worlds for quite some time.

Not one to upset her impulsive, temperamental

son, Jeanne rarely, if ever, questioned him about his nighttime wanderings, the countless unfinished projects, or even the layers of debris that covered every inch of his room. Joel loves his mother dearly, but concedes that at the time she was the least of his worries. Jeanne kept herself busy with her own pursuits, namely gardening, traveling, early morning Tai Chi sessions, and socializing with friends. Meanwhile, when Joel, who was always as nervous as he was unkempt and disorganized, was alone he would imagine the furtive eyes of the local police force watching his every move as they prepared to pounce on him for killing Susie. With that at the forefront of his mind, his mother was of little concern to him.

As afraid as he was about getting caught, Joel could not keep himself from returning to the city streets, which had become his devil's playground. Even before his mother's return from Colorado, he was back seeking the services of hookers, though he insists he went to great lengths to ensure that Susie was not only his first victim but his last. He vowed never to commit another homicide and made what he still perceives as a noble effort to keep that promise. "I just didn't want to do it again," he said. "Within a week I was in a hotel room with somebody. That is probably why I was in a hotel room. Because in a hotel room it [was] less likely to happen."

Despite the fact that he was once again cavorting with prostitutes, the discovery of Susie's head made Joel even more afraid of being found out. "It [the killing] was a tense memory," he said. "There were times that I got very anxious about it. There were times it was pleasurable. I remember for like a month checking every car in the neighborhood. I knew the cars. These people own a white car and a red car, and these people own a blue car and an orange car. If there were any strange cars in the neighborhood I would get a little nervous."

Although many experts insist he is not being truthful, Joel swears that he never consciously felt any real sense of empowerment, exhilaration, or even accomplishment during his murderous spree. "No, no, it wasn't like that," he asserted. But some of his non-lethal actions suggest otherwise. Very often he would pick the most strung-out, desperate-looking girl on the street, invite her into his vehicle, then waste fifteen or twenty minutes of her time before declining her services. "I didn't realize it was [empowerment] until I did some reading on it," he said. "Even approaching [the girl], going through the whole pattern, she does her little sales pitch, and then you drive off. She waits for the next car. Yeah, I guess that's empowerment. But I didn't really feel it then, but I know now it was because it's been labeled for me."

Whether he realized it then or not, with the

murder of Susie he was finally in charge of something: his destiny, as well as the destiny of the scores of victims and potential victims who would cross his path over the next four years. "Once Rifkin committed his first homicide, the monster within him was in effect hatched," said Joseph A. Piraino, a retired NYPD sergeant and current civilian investigator for the Manhattan district attorney's office who also received specialized training at the FBI National Academy in Quantico, Virginia. A graduate degree candidate in forensic psychology, Piraino is an expert on the subject of serial killing. "We don't know much about his genetic background because of the fact that he was adopted, but it is usually safe to assume there was a predisposition toward psychopathic behavior. Most times we see that manifest itself early on through juvenile delinquency. Not all people with that predisposition act on their impulses, but many do. In Rifkin's mind his aggressive behavior enabled him to win the women he could never have normally, to conquer them.

"Under normal conditions, he would have met no shortage of obstacles in just meeting women," continued Piraino. "But under pathological conditions he was able to express himself completely by subduing and totally controlling the object of his desire, then destroying it. In essence the only time he could function 'normally,' in his mind at least, was when he was behaving pathologically. And once the monster was hatched, it was impossible for him to control his impulses. He now had a road map where his destinations were already plotted. All he had to do was follow the trip plan. Each victim became like a new city to travel to."

WHILE JOEL SAYS THE MEMORY Of SUSIE'S demise would replay in his head over and over like a porn loop on automatic pilot, he insists it did not provide the sexual enhancement that forensic experts insist it must have. And he gets extremely upset over the fact that some psychiatrists persist in suggesting that his level of arousal was greatly intensified by the act of killing. The way he says he remembers it, the opposite was actually true. By the time he killed Susie he felt in desperate need of something, anything, to make him feel alive. No longer would engaging in sex with prostitutes, sometimes five in one night, satisfy his needs. He needed more stimulation. For the first time ever, his sexual addiction was now controlling him.

"It didn't enhance my life," he said. "I knew that

my repeated going to the streets was becoming a multiple problem. It was a personal problem, it was a health problem, it was a financial problem. I mean it was controlling my life. I didn't know the term sexual addiction then, but I do now and I was absolutely addicted to the streets. I had done all kinds of robbing Peter to pay Paul. My fix was the streets. When you really hit bottom you fight against the bottom. I think [by killing] I was trying to just make the streets so that they were not attractive to me anymore."

Joel steadfastly maintains that he had no deep-rooted hatred for women in general or prostitutes in particular, but was only trying to stem his overpowering and degrading need for their sexual services. According to him, they had to die so he could, in essence, kill his reliance on them. It was obvious that he chose to date prostitutes so he could avoid rejection. Perhaps they even helped Joel convince himself that he did not actually need a woman for a relationship. Like a single person who only dates married people, there is a certain degree of safety in only attaching one's self to those who are unavailable.

"Just going to the streets made me feel negative," he said. "I had regular girlfriends, but they were few and far between. The idea that I just asked somebody for a date and she said no, [I would think] 'what's wrong with me, what am I doing wrong, have

I got three heads or something?' That type of thing. And then you go to the street and you're like this is the only way. I just can't be normal."

Joel's graduation to murder was like a cocaine sniffer switching from powder to the infinitely more potent crack. In an attempt to destroy his need for consumer sex, he had developed an even more insatiable and destructive desire for murder. He was frightened and repulsed by the fact that only thoughts of killing made him feel alive. Like a person trying to stop overeating or overindulging in alcohol, Joel began writing little daily reminders to himself, such as "no more p[rostitutes], no more k[illing]." But he was not doing this out of any great concern for his potential victims; he was as much afraid of getting caught as he was of being controlled by another even more dangerous addiction.

As time went on, Joel said that the murderous loops dancing in his head sometimes served as a stimulant, sometimes as a downer, and sometimes just as a seemingly inconsequential recurring thought pattern. It got to the point where he did not particularly welcome them. Because killing excited him more than sex now, he found himself fantasizing about killing nearly every girl he was with. Very often fighting the urge to kill would diminish his ability to maintain an erection. "[Often] I would start to sexually lose it and pass it off as I drank too much tonight or was up too late type of thing," he explained. "[Then I would] pay the girl off and drop her off. Other times I would play the loop and it wouldn't bother me at all. I would have a great time with the girl."

Although he had vowed never to kill again, a year and a half after Susie's death, he found himself in a similar position. His mother went away on yet another trip, and he brought another streetwalker from the Jamaica Avenue stroll back to the family home. Throughout the day, the two of them left on several occasions so she could score drugs. Unbeknownst to Joel, every time she left the house the woman was pilfering jewelry from his mother's bedroom. "She was in and out of the house three or four times," he recalled. "She basically cleaned the house out and I didn't even know about it. And we never actually had sex either."

Jeanne Rifkin was livid when she returned home and discovered her possessions missing. Joel was forced to confess his proclivities, which both shocked and angered his mother. But like her son, she was able to compartmentalize his actions and not become consumed by her deep disappointment and anger. "[Of course] she blamed me," said Joel. "Who the hell brings a prostitute to the house and then lets her roam around the house by herself? [She was] very angry. She's still probably angry over it."

Not long afterward, in a period Joel refers to as "a weird time," he met another Jamaica Avenue hooker named Charlene to whom he related his theft tale. Vowing that she would try to help him, she left his car and returned minutes later with his father's college ring, which he did not even know was missing. "She went into a crack house, saw it, bought it back, or stole it back," he said. The grateful Joel, who would have been too cowardly to attempt retrieving the jewelry on his own, took pity on his benefactor when "she mentioned that she had all these things to do and no way of doing [them]. I said well, I wasn't doing anything and agreed to drive her upstate. I drove her to detox twice, I drove her to see her kid, too."

While his benevolent actions toward Charlene might have indicated that his heart was softening a bit, Joel was still feeling angry and betrayed when it came to the women of the streets. One night in late 1990, when his mother was once again out of town, he spotted a doe-eyed woman named Julie Blackbird under the Manhattan Bridge. After she agreed to accompany him home, he drove her to bucolic East Meadow. "She had this pseudo-Madonna look to her," recalled Joel. "She had these plastic wrist bands, the whole bit. [She was] dressed like she had just come out of one of the clubs."

After a night of sexual revelry, capped off by a

few hours of MTV, Joel drove Julie to a local ATM at seven in the morning to withdraw the extra money he had promised her. All night he had resisted the urge to kill her. But Joel became upset when the ATM spit out a notice that his account contained insufficient funds for withdrawal. "I had made a deposit in the bank and as far as I knew the money was there," he said. "I promised X amount of money, I had X amount of money. I go to the ATM [and] it's like no, you don't have any money."

Joel and Julie returned to his home to wait for the bank to open two hours later. It was not until they were almost out the door that he could no longer resist the urge to strike. "And this time it was a much heavier object [I used], because the howitzer shell no longer existed," he said. "[It was] a table leg or something. Or sawed-off bat. We had these table legs. For a period my mom was redoing furniture, so we'd keep old scrap wood."

It is crucial for him to point out that, in his mind at least, the circumstances of Julie's death, as well as those of the subsequent deaths, prove that he did not act with premeditation, but as a result of some primal impulse that was beyond his control. If that was so, I wondered, why had he been able to resist the strong urge to kill for the past year and a half? Was he prompted to kill again because he was wronged by the thieving woman, or perhaps because his feelings had softened recently toward Charlene? Was he afraid of losing his power by placing himself in such a vulnerable position? Was he afraid he was going to once again become the butt of a joke? Joel seemed annoyed by my questions, not because they were meddling, but because they were upsetting the rhythm of his storytelling.

"I had fantasized about it and dismissed it [all night]," he continued. "I was in control of myself. Then we go back to the house [after the ATM machine] and we sit around the house for two more hours, so the whole thing started all over again. And this time I couldn't control it, [I had gotten] a second shot at it. If the money had come out of that machine we would have been on the parkway and we would have gone to the city and she would have lived. I'm ninety-nine percent sure of that."

IMMEDIATELY AFTER BLUDGEONING JULIE
to death, Joel remembers "completely bugging out." This loss of control had nothing to do with the sudden realization of how bestial he had become—nor was it related to any deeply rooted sense of remorse. Once again it had only to do with getting caught and the grisly logistics of disposing of the body. The neophyte killer began to experience a powerful sense of foreboding and gloom, and his fear got to the point where he was thinking irrationally, perhaps insanely.

"We had this flash flooding type of thing, and they found certain parts I thought they would never find," Joel recalled vexatiously. "[That] fit one of my little phobic theories, with energy forces and stuff like that. When a guy hits a golf ball and the ball slices like you have never seen it slice before, rolls down a hill, and rolls right by a certain body part, I was like, okay, what caused the golf ball to do these crazy things? So yeah, it makes you paranoid, [I was going to make sure] this wasn't [going to happen] a second time."

Determined to make sure Julie's body would never surface as a result of cosmic forces, or any other force of nature for that matter, he did not rush to formulate a disposal plan. Because he still had several days until his mother returned from her trip, he decided to get some rest and let things fall into place later on. Trying to figure out a plan that would keep him from getting caught and spending the rest of his life in prison would have to wait until his body was rested, his head was cleared, and his emotions were settled. First things first, he told himself as he carried Julie's rigid body into the basement. He did not wrap it or cover it or even try to put it out of view.

Then Joel retired to his upstairs bedroom and fell into a deep, restful sleep. Awakening several hours later, he was amazed to find that a plan had taken shape in his head while he slept. "I went to the local Home Depot, bought a mortar pan, quick cement, X-Acto knife, and did what I did with the first one," he said. "Except this time the packages were placed in cement."

When I asked how an X-Acto knife could be

used to chop a head off, especially when so many muscles, ligaments, and tendons would have to be cut through, Joel looked at me incredulously. "It works just like a scalpel," he intoned as if giving a lesson on the rudiments of dismemberment was as normal as giving directions to a lost motorist. "[With] the first girl [I used] the little one with the triangular blade. The second one was [one of] those cheap orange ones with the blades that slide up and down. If you use a long length, it will snap. So I always used a little [bit of the blade], like a scalpel. I did it on the floor and then mopped it up, but there wasn't that much [blood]. When there is no heart rate it doesn't flow and after it co-agulates it stays where it is, basically. It thickens. I had no idea beforehand. It was one of the things I learned afterwards."

Once again I found myself struggling with my ability to be objective. How, I wondered, could I have ever compared myself to Joel, who was de-scribing things in sickeningly clinical detail that I was completely incapable of imagining, much less acting upon? Adding to my confusion was the fact that although he did not act or look like an insane man, Joel was talking freely in a way I thought only an insane person would. For the first time I suspected I had come face to face with pure evil, which was something I had always argued did not exist.

After dissecting the body, he placed most of the parts in cement; then, realizing that it had to dry, he waited for two days. "I was too paranoid to hang out anymore. In her case there was three [packages]. I put the two arms in one bucket and the two legs in [a] pan. And the head in another bucket. The torso, I couldn't do that with, so that was wrapped in a milk crate and I think that ended up in the Hudson River."

Having read about serial killer Ted Bundy's sexual proclivities with the bodies of his deceased victims, Joel says he briefly considered having sex with Julie but quickly changed his mind. "I had heard of necrophilia and the thought popped in [my head], and the thought got rejected," he said unconvincingly. "I just remember looking down at her and thinking about it. I am looking at her and I'm like 'Nah.' And that was it, never had the thought again. I was like, no, I don't see how people could ever do that."

If those words are to be believed, it is truly remarkable how disturbed he can get over the thought of himself or others having sex with someone they just killed and dismembered, while the thought of taking their life had no effect at all. Although numerous mental health experts would raise this question during many interviews over the next few years, Joel constantly and wholeheartedly rejected the notion that he derived sexual pleasure from any of his dead victims. But when the police searched his home after his arrest, they found numerous news clippings and magazine articles chronicling the exploits of Bundy and the still unapprehended Green River Killer in the Pacific Northwest, both of whom were necrophiliacs.

"I think I imitated what I read, because a lot of what I told [the psychiatrists] is almost lifted page by page from the [Green River] book," said Joel. "He buried one, I buried one. He went from water to land, I went from water to land. He placed one by an airport, I placed one by an airport. He did things in clusters, I did things in clusters."

Joel admits to taking numerous cues from his counterparts and copying many of their obsessive habits, yet he denies extracting pleasure from his lifeless victims. His strong denials reminded me of a drug addict who insists he would never stoop to using needles, as if he were following a code of ethics for objectionable behavior. Joel seemed to be saying he could explain away his murderous actions just as long as he did not have sex with the corpses. To a sane and rational human being, this so-called morality only made his crimes all the more egregious.

After dismembering the corpse Joel encountered another dilemma: what to do with all of her possessions. Unlike most streetwalkers, Julie did not travel light. Her jewelry alone could fill a sack. Joel did not even realize how much he had kept until later, when the police claimed he was collecting souvenirs from all of his victims for nostalgia purposes. "There was just so much of it that through the disposal I had to take this stuff off and it was like 'all right, I'll come back and take care of this [later],'" he recalled. "And I didn't. And then through reading the [book about] the Green River [killer], I heard about taking souvenirs and trophies so I just kept the stuff. I don't know if I kept [stuff] from every girl, but the majority I would say, a good eighty percent."

After putting Julie's remains in his car, Joel headed into the city to discard them. Along the way, he even went by some of his regular strolls. "I was driving around and had one [of the cement packages] on the floor of the front seat of the car," he recalled almost wistfully. "I was talking to a girl and debating whether I should pick her up."

Still a bit spooked by the fact that Susie's head had been discovered, Joel was much more thoughtful about dumping Julie's body parts where he was certain they would never turn up. "I really got insane about her not being found," he said. After much careful thought he dumped the head and torso into the Hudson River at different locations, and the arms and legs in an old barge canal in Brooklyn. Much of her personal property, including a diary, was recovered in Joel's bedroom after his arrest.

When told that most people would be spooked just hearing about such cruel and morbid behavior, Joel responded in a stiff, almost businesslike manner, as if he were explaining to a neighbor how he rid his lawn of pesky dandelions. "I looked at it as a job," he said. "Like, okay, this is what you gotta do now. Do this and that to make it smaller so you can get rid of it. I did it."

In the months after Julie's murder, Joel brought several women home to East Meadow, all of whom he later returned unharmed. After about four months of enhancing these evenings with nothing more than his murderous memories, the lethal Lothario struck again. Once again, it was in the comfort of the family home while his mother was away. The victim was thirty-one-year-old, five-foot, three-inch Barbara Jacobs, whose last known address was in Queens and who had an arrest record for prostitution and auto theft. He picked her up at East 12th Street and Second Avenue in July 1991.

"I didn't have a plan for the third one," he said. "We watched TV a little bit. She wanted to get some rest. I was in the house just rambling around, so it wasn't a sudden thing. I am debating with myself, I am like No and Yes and I ended up on Yes and I hit her. I clubbed her again like the first two. She was sleeping."

Although worn thin from years of drug abuse, Jacobs was not knocked unconscious from the initial attack and put up a valiant effort for her life. "We ended up wrestling on the floor and I strangled her," Joel recalled emotionlessly. After dragging Jacobs's body into the basement so he could cut it up and prepare it for disposal, an odd thing, even by Joel's abnormal standards, occurred. It still perplexes him.

"Her I couldn't dissect," he said almost irritably. "For some reason I could not do it." Asked if what he had experienced was perhaps remorse or a bout of emotional recoil, he seemed genuinely stumped. "I don't know, I just couldn't," he repeated. "I mean I had everything to do it, [but] I didn't start. I got to the point where I was ready to cut. I had the knife in my hand and I'm looking at the body and *eghhhh*. [I told myself] I'll come back and do this later."

After a while, Joel wrapped the body in plastic, placed it in a cardboard box, put it in the back of his mother's four-door blue Toyota sedan, and headed for the city to scope out a dump site. He drove around for quite some time before picking what turned out to be a dangerous location.

"There was a cement processing [plant] on the Hudson [River]," he said. "Had I been thinking about my surroundings, that would have been the last place I would have chosen. Down the piers there was a training exercise with the fire department. I could see all the lights and [knew] that is [where] the current was headed, and they were the people who found it."

Afterward, Joel dawdled about the city, even stopping to purchase oral sex from a prostitute. He was halfway home when he heard on the car radio that Jacobs's body had just been found. Because he had dumped it just hours earlier, he was amazed at how uncharacteristically calm he was. "It didn't even faze me," he said. To this day he is surprised he did not have a panic attack.

None of Jacobs's family members could be contacted and she was buried in a cemetery for unclaimed bodies. But after Joel confessed to her murder, Jacobs's father was located and he had the body moved to a Jewish cemetery on Long Island where she received a more suitable spiritual burial.

The calm Joel experienced after the discovery of Jacobs's body did not last long. He again began to fear getting arrested and for reasons he still finds inexplicable, kept thinking about the effect his actions would have had on his father had he lived long enough to learn about them. Having lived for so long in the shadow of his father, and having always been so eager to please him, he could not come to grips with the behavior he was certain would have had his father convulsing in his grave.

Unlike his mother, whom he considers the ultimate survivor, Joel is certain his father would have severed all ties with him, moved out of the neighborhood he loved because of his inability to face the neighbors, and escaped into a tortured solitary world. Much to the detriment of all the victims to follow, that twinge of conscience or concern did not last long.

While Joel may have found a way to live with his actions, he still knew that he was headed for disaster if he persisted in his killing. Maybe the cops would never link him to the first three but he was sure that if he continued it was only a matter of time before he slipped up. "After the third I realized that this is a problem," he explained. "It's not gonna go away. There is no one I can really talk to about it. I just have to deal with it."

Joel fleetingly thought about seeking some type of counseling, but quickly realized that any admissions of murder would not be protected by doctor-client privilege. A few years later, a Westchester County, New York, man was convicted of a double murder he had committed years earlier in the midst of a drug- and alcohol-induced stupor. His conviction was based largely on statements he had made at an Alcoholics Anonymous meeting. After months of fierce, protracted pre-trial suppression hearings it was determined that the sanctity of an AA meeting might cover comments related to adultery or embezzlement, but certainly not murder.

"Society, the way it's set up, really can't [help you]," lamented Joel, who was implying that it was unjust that there was no twelve-step program for serial murderers as there was for alcoholics, drug addicts, and co-dependents. "Even the clergy, as much as they say that they can keep total confidence, [they can't]. And even psychiatrists, when people confess to horrendous crimes there's no help out there. It's okay, you have a problem, we'll lock you up. I'm sure you've done it in your line of work, and I just think it's so funny when [people in] law enforcement always say 'we'll try and get you help. Just tell us, you know, what's going on. We can help you.' Well, a six-by-nine [cell] is not exactly help."

Ray Pierce is a retired detective who spent twenty-eight years with the NYPD. After receiving an FBI fellowship in psychological profiling with the behavioral science unit at the FBI National Academy in 1985, he became a nationally renowned expert on criminal profiling, as well as the architect of the department's criminal assessment and profiling unit. He now runs a consulting firm, RMP International, in Yonkers, New York. He has no doubt that Joel genuinely views himself as a hopeless addict and blames society for his murderous actions. "Through all the years he was bombarded with abuse, Rifkin built a wall around him that finally evolved into a sense of entitlement that grew deadly," Pierce explained. "I think he believed 'after what I went through, I now have the right to display my power. As powerless as I am in life, killing enables me to manipulate and control.' Joel was an impulsive person to begin with, so when the killing started that impulsivity was unleashed even more. It was really not much different from a drug addict chasing a high. He developed an addiction to killing."

While, in his own head, Joel may have found a way to justify the killing of his first three victims, he did not have to work hard for a rationalization when it came to the fourth. One night around Labor Day weekend in 1991, he was on one of his semi-regular three-hour pilgrimages, with no predisposition whatsoever toward murder. Although he was thinking about it, as he always was, the urge to strike was not particularly strong that night. He was more interested in what he called window shopping. "There was a way, if I wanted to take all night to get some place, I could start at Hempstead Turnpike [on Long Island], check out a stroll in the village of Hempstead, continue up to around Belmont [Raceway in Queens], check out another stroll by the track, hook on to Jamaica [Avenue in Queens], there were a couple of strolls there, go on to Atlantic [Avenue in Brooklyn], come across the bridge and hit Allen and Forsythe Streets and First and Second Avenues [all in Manhattan], go up to Forty-second [Street in midtown Manhattan], loop back down through [the Jacob] Javits Center [on West 33rd Street and Ninth Avenue], then cut across First and Second Avenues again."

After finding nothing of interest in his price range, Joel was headed home when he made one last pass through the Jamaica Avenue stroll. Even though he had picked up women there before, it was far from his favorite stroll and he was uncomfortable doing business there. But he was immediately smitten by the curly hair and exotic Mediterranean looks of Mary Ellen DeLuca. One of four daughters, DeLuca had grown up in a close-knit Italian family but had started using drugs in high school. Over the next few years she tried her hand at being a manicurist, a singer, and a computer student, but always wound up back on drugs and out on the street. In the darkness she could easily have passed for Hispanic, and Joel liked her olive skin and non-threatening demeanor. He had hoped for a quick fix before turning in for the evening, but wound up getting much more than he had anticipated.

"She was chasing [drugs] all night," Joel recalled. "This was a con I have gotten a number of times, and I have been stupid enough to [continually] fall into it." Joel drove her to numerous buying locations and was beginning to get frustrated. "She was on rock cocaine, she smoked the whole thing and [started] hitting on the resin," he said. "All she wants to do is get high. [She gets this] neurosis, where [she] starts looking at everything, digging in the carpet, digging everywhere, [she thinks she] dropped a rock somewhere. So she finishes that. And then she says 'we have been here too long, let's go to another place,' which made sense to me. I pass another spot, she gets high again. So we are doing this for ten hours."

Joel had already shelled out about $150, and they still had not had sex yet. Finally, at dawn, he told her, " 'Hey, it's sunrise, the day has begun, it has been nice hanging out with you, hit the road.' And she gets all upset. 'Well, this time, I promise, we'll do the date,' [she said]. I say I'm out of money and she says 'well, if you can get more money . . .' "

Describing himself as a dumb slug, Joel dropped off DeLuca at a strip mall in front of a sleazy, short-stay motel just a few miles from his home, then pulled a few cons of his own. At the time he was the proprietor of a small, struggling landscaping company and had leased a fenced-in, twenty-by-fifty-foot Hicksville, Long Island, lot from a man who ran a very successful landscaping design and tree service. It was only supposed to be used for storing his broken-down trailer and rusty, outdated gardening equipment. Joel often feuded with the landlord about paying the rent on time, and the landlord was amazed that Joel, whom he saw as utterly shiftless, was even able to stay in business. He could not even hold onto the weekly customers for whom he did nothing more than mow their lawns. But the landlord never suspected that Joel was a criminal, much less a murderer, or that his property would be used as a temporary depot for dead bodies on their way to being dumped elsewhere.

When Joel arrived there on this morning, his only employee was waiting for him. "I end up telling him, 'oh man, I was out partying all night,' which was half truth half lie," said Joel. "No way I could work that day, I'm shot. I run the same type of line against my mom. I pick up some money, money that I either had to pay the [worker] with or had to buy equipment with. But it's cash. It no longer has a designation anymore, it was just money. It was enough to pay for the room, pay for her."

Once they were ensconced in the motel, things did not get any better. "She started with the let-me-get-high-first [routine]," Joel said. "And she didn't want to do it [have sex]. And then when we are doing it, she is like 'Are you done yet? Done yet? Done yet?' It was a whole bad scene."

Joel became even more agitated when DeLuca began complaining about how much she hated her life and how she just wished she could end it. He asked her repeatedly if she was being truthful, if she truly wanted to die. When DeLuca answered in the affirmative, he climbed on top of her and strangled her to death without so much as a passing thought. Oddly enough, she put up no resistance. "That was one of the weird ones," he said. "She was awake, [but did] nothing, just like accepted it."

The DeLuca killing is another of the many examples he uses as the basis for his vehement contention that there was never any premeditation on his part. "If I was gonna premeditate, it would have [been] some place isolated," he explained. "Because [now] I had a double problem. The hotel manager sees two people go into a room, sees one person leave. And how do I get the body out? Plus I was on the video tape, plus he had my [license] plate number when I rented the room."

Remembering that a steamer trunk had been used to store a body in the film *Frenzy*, Joel drove to a nearby Kmart and picked one up. "I managed to fit her into that," he said. He also concocted a complex story, replete with props, in case he was questioned by the clerk. "[It was] a whole big elaborate thing, where I would bring empty luggage in and out of the room," he explained. "[Then] I went in with this big thing and came out with it on a hand truck. That is when I talked with the manager and gave him some bull crap about driving some stuff upstate."

Joel did in fact drive upstate, to the quaint village of Cornwall in Orange County, a stone's throw from West Point. He pulled off to the side of the road near a picnic area and a hot dog truck and deposited DeLuca's body at a dump site. He even took the time to take her out of the trunk; it would eventually be the final resting place for victim number five.

It did not take long for DeLuca's loving family, who had admitted her to drug rehabs on numerous occasions in the past, to start looking for their errant daughter. They reported her missing to the police, then scoured drug dens in Queens on their own, showing her picture to anyone who would look at it. But all of their efforts would be for naught. Less than a month later, on October 1, her decomposed body, wearing only a bra, was found. Since her body could not be identified, it was buried in a grave marked Jane Doe.

OVER THE NEXT FEW WEEKS, WHILE JOEL was with several prostitutes, he harmed none of them. He actually gave himself credit for being so good because, as always, thoughts of killing occupied his mind. One afternoon, just an hour after having a sexual encounter with another woman, he picked up thirty-one-year-old Korean-born Yun Lee in his truck on the Allen Street stroll in the shadow of the Williamsburg Bridge. Joel, who usually preferred oral sex, desired actual intercourse that day. He insists that, as with his other victims, he had no plan to kill the slight and seemingly sweet Lee, whom he had dated before and who had been arrested eleven times for prostitution and narcotics possession. Joel drove to a pier along the East River, near the New York *Post* building, but was thwarted by the multitude of homeless encampments that dotted the waterfront.

"There were a lot of squat villages," he recalled. "Between them there [were] some blank spots and some cars. We went there first."

Because the area was such a hub of activity, Joel soon moved to a more deserted area closer to the bridge, though he continued to feel uncomfortable. Adding to his woes was his inability to achieve an erection, probably because he had just had sex an hour earlier. "That was one of the first ones where I couldn't do anything," he said. "I played it off as there are too many people, there is too much happening around here. [So] we [moved] to a parking lot where you can probably park illegally. And we parked among the cars and started again."

Although Lee never got completely undressed, she prepared herself for vehicular sex in what Joel describes as typical hooker fashion. "In the car they will basically take one leg out of the pants," he marveled. "They are very good at getting in and out of situations where even if someone rolls up on you during the act, by the time you address the person they are like nothing happened. They are very good at it. It is one of the neat things about the street crowd."

But Joel could still not maintain an erection and began getting more and more agitated. While he does not recall being driven to the point of extreme anger, he does remember killing Lee without so much as a fleeting thought or the slightest provocation. He struck without warning, like a poisonous snake on an unsuspecting camper. "I just grabbed her by the throat, and that was that," he said. Although it was still daylight, Joel drove back to Long Island with the body lying next to him on the passenger seat. He headed straight for his work lot, where his steamer trunk was stored. "I put her in the trunk, and put the trunk in the back [of the truck]," he recalled. "And I think that night I disposed of her."

Heading back into the city, Joel drove to a deserted area in the South Bronx, not far from the Triboro Bridge. "There was this road that dead-ended at the [Harlem] River," he said. "There was no barrier, no nothing, and there was a fenced-in parking lot on one side and a factory on the other side and it was pretty isolated. I remember pitching it into the river and it floating away." The body, still stuffed in the trunk, was found several months later, floating down the Harlem River between East 123rd Street and Randalls Island.

At the time, Joel did not stop to think of the emerging pattern in his killings. All seemed to occur in the wake of a perceived slight or following either a real or imagined humiliation. There was the thievery or indifference of the hookers, his own kindness toward Charlene which he might have later interpreted as weakness, his failures at attaining or maintaining erections.

Asked if he could have been angered by his inability to perform sexually, his almost muted response was "could be," although it was obvious he was not convinced that was the answer. "It didn't fit the pattern, this wasn't a total stranger type of thing," he said. Although Lee would be the first of Joel's victims whom he had dated beforehand, she would not be the last. While he described her as normally friendly, on the day of their final rendezvous Joel recalls her being "a little more stressed." He then implies that he construed her frazzled demeanor as a sign of disrespect, almost acting as if it were her fault he became homicidal. "She may have needed to go pop [shoot up], but she was too polite to go pop first," he said. "That type of thing."

Soon afterward, Joel realized that the death of Lee had left an indelible impression on him. Not only had he purchased her services several times prior to their fatal encounter, he had also developed some positive feelings toward her. She was unable to speak as he was choking her, but she looked at him quizzically, Joel recalled, then "mouthed something about making a big mistake." He was never fearful of a vengeful pimp coming after him or having to live with his own conscience or even having to pay an exorbitant spiritual price for his actions once he crossed over to the other side upon his own death. As self-absorbed as he always was, Joel says he was fairly certain "she was referring to herself," meaning she made the mistake. "Then again," he added almost as an afterthought, "she could have meant a pimp and I just, you know, turned it around. Once you get into a certain mode, you just respond to very little."

My blood began to boil at this comment, and I came very close to losing my cool. Having just confessed to killing five women in cold blood, Joel conveniently found a way to lay the blame, in some small way, on all of them. Had he seemed crazy it would have been easier for me to tolerate. But he seemed as sane as I, even as he disavowed personal responsibility for every crime he ever committed. I realized later that as angry as I was at him, I was also very annoyed with myself. What did I expect from the confessed killer of seventeen prostitutes? Had I naively believed that I could get Joel to bare his soul and proclaim to me how troubled he was by his actions? If so, it was now apparent that I would be greatly disappointed. The truth was, Joel wasn't troubled in the least.

Sensing the change in my demeanor, I think Joel tried to soften his image but was incredibly unconvincing in doing so. What confounded him more than anything else, he repeated, was the fact that he even killed Lee in the first place. He insisted that he genuinely regretted taking her life. "This was a girl I had been with [several] times before," he said. "Actually, I thought I liked [her]. That's why I had been with her more than once."

Joel slowed down for several months after the Lee murder and did not strike again until shortly before the 1991 Christmas season. He picked up a woman whose name he can't recall, then strangled her during sex in his truck. He would eventually plead guilty to her murder; her identity was officially listed as Jane Doe. While he remembers little about her, he does recall picking her up on the West 46th Street stroll, between Eighth and Ninth Avenues. The beautiful, tree-lined street is known as Restaurant Row because both sides are lined with trendy eateries that cater to the Broadway theater crowd. In the late eighties and early nineties, however, the area was a notorious cruising strip and a haven for lawlessness. The proprietors of the restaurants, who saw their profits steadily declining, were at their wits' end trying to stop it. Prostitutes trolled the street at all hours of the day and night, brazen drug dealers openly sold their wares, and junkies freely robbed the never-ending stream of tourists and theater-goers who wandered onto the perilous turf.

Even though at the time over two thousand people a year were being murdered throughout the city's five boroughs, many officials threw up their hands in disgust at the runaway crime epidemic and did little to combat it. A sense of social disorder gripped the city, and no one in power was doing anything to change it. In a last-ditch effort to salvage their businesses, restaurant owners began paying off a local vigilante group to rid the area of this scourge of miscreants. Unlike the police, the hired muscle, donned in uniforms, saw themselves as true saviors of society and roughed up the local criminals, dumped their drugs, and chased them from the streets. But once the theaters emptied and the restaurants closed, it was back to business as usual. In the late hours of the night, when all was quiet, it was one of Joel's favorite strolls. Having spent so much time downtown, he welcomed the change and loved the excitement of Broadway, even long after the evening's final curtains. After picking up his latest victim, he drove to a nearby parking lot. "And during the [oral] sex act, [I] strangled her," he said emotionlessly.

Asked if he had trouble performing that night, he grew annoyed and dismissive. "I don't know, I don't know if we even got that far," he answered tersely. "But I just remember it was very quick." While he remembers little about the murder of this faceless victim, he remembers the aftermath all too well. He still gets goose bumps thinking about how close he came to getting caught that night.

Joel drove back to Long Island with the body lying in the front seat of the truck. It was not the first time he had done such a foolish thing, nor would it be the last. After each killing Joel would go through what he called a "logic phase," which could best be described as a lack-of-logic phase. Having a dead body in the front seat of one's vehicle was about as far from logical as one could get. "I didn't necessarily associate it with being a body," he said. "[With] one of the [later] girls, I [even] stopped at a gas station with [her in the front seat], got out, pre-paid, and pumped the gas. Other times I am on the Long Island Expressway, with trucks [that] have a high cab. Nothing was cranking logically, I guess."

Joel delivered the body to his landscaping lot and quickly and quietly stored his latest victim under a tarp. That afternoon he remembered that a recycling company in nearby Westbury, where he had done some temp work in the past, stored empty steel drums on their own lot. "So I basically stole a fifty-five-gallon drum," he confessed. He stuffed the woman into the drum, then drove to an area in upper Manhattan or the South Bronx where there were many abandoned cars, junk yards, and chop shops. Pulling off to the side of the road Joel quickly muscled the drum to the edge of the water. "I got the body to the water, it hit the water because I heard a splash," he recalled.

To his horror, when he turned around he found himself face to face with two patrolmen who had been alerted to his presence by an anonymous 911 call. "They thought someone was doing some illegal dumping," he explained, oblivious of his ghastly pun. "And I very quickly said 'no, I'm scavenging.' And they said, 'what?' And I said 'well, there was an abandoned car at the side [of the road], not too far from where I parked. My understanding is if I scavenge off that [car] I get arrested, but if I scavenge off this lot, it is clean money [because I'm] clearing the litter.' "

Taking the charade a step further, Joel picked up an axle for a prop and told the officers, "I can get about thirty bucks for this." Once Joel had rolled it onto the back of his truck, the cops suggested he go scavenge someplace else. When told that he was pretty quick on his feet for someone usually so nervous, he seemed both elated and embarrassed at the compliment. "It comes from years of lying," he said sheepishly.

When asked if he was proud of the con he had pulled, he replied: "I didn't dare to think about it at that point. I just got in the car and made sure the seatbelt was on and the directional was on as I was pulling out at a nice rate of speed. Because I was completely paralyzed." As always, Joel's paralysis did not last long.

Because many of the victims' bodies were found long after the murders, it is often difficult to determine exactly when they were killed. While Joel acknowledges that he is "terrible with dates" (he could not even remember with certainty the date of his father's death) his chronology of the killings was similar during each interview I had with him, and the general facts surrounding them remained the same. But when describing his actions after number six, Joel explained, "this is one of the times where the whole videotape is blurry as far as order." While there is no way to determine with total accuracy the order of the next several killings, I have used news accounts, Joel's recollections, and other investigative data in chronicling them.

Joel does not remember feeling any more melancholy than usual that Christmas season. On December 26, he canceled plans to celebrate with his pinochle friends, opting instead to embark on one of his frequent prowls. It did not take him long to spot Lorraine Orvieto on a dank street in a rundown section of Bayshore, Long Island. Orvieto was a twenty-eight-year-old former cheerleader who grew up in a seemingly ideal Long Island household but was besieged with a host of personal and emotional problems. After graduating from high school she spent eight years living at home but was diagnosed with manic-depression at the age of twenty-five. She began using cocaine to control her constantly changing moods, and soon developed a fierce crack habit. Just months before being killed she had been hospitalized at the nearby Kings Park Psychiatric Center, then moved into an outpatient home in Bayshore. Six days before her death she phoned her parents to say she was having problems and would not see them for a while. There is every indication that she turned to prostitution full-time.

A small town on the south shore, Bayshore is best known as the ferry hub for day trippers en route to Fire Island. While much of the town has an idyllic New England charm, it also has a rough edge. There is no shortage of poverty, nor is the community a stranger to crime. Bayshore is home to several well-known strolls and Joel, of course, was familiar with all of them. Once he picked up Orvieto, things progressed quickly. "We went to a schoolyard, parked along a fence, and [I choked her] in the middle of the [oral] sex act." Upon rifling through her belongings, Joel was nonplussed to discover that the woman he had just killed had HIV. "She had a big brown pharmacy bottle of AZT," he said. "That was one of the things I kept [as a souvenir]."

Joel's nonchalance about contracting a potentially deadly sexually transmitted disease (STD) would change in a hurry soon afterward. Like so many other men, he believed it was nearly impossible to contract AIDS from oral sex, regardless of the physical condition of the carrier. He was so used to living with herpes and other STDs that he had stopped feeling any particular stress. But the reason he gave for wearing a condom during most of his dates sounds unbelievable. "So she [the prostitute] didn't get it, and the next guy didn't get it, and the next guy [after that]," he said. "The fact that I used one sometimes was irrelevant. If the girl wanted to use one, yeah [I would]."

Soon after killing Orvieto, Joel transported her body to the work lot where it was stored before being stuffed into a drum. He eventually dumped it in a murky inlet at Coney Island, Brooklyn, some forty miles away, where it was found by a fisherman on July 11, 1992. Later, when the Orvieto family initiated a wrongful death lawsuit against Joel, his reaction was viewed by many observers as complete derangement. Acting as if he actually had something to lose should the judgment go against him, he lashed into the family with a vindictive handwritten response. Once again he blamed the victim for her own demise and coldly implied that her life was not worth living and that her parents had no right to be upset about her death. He described Lorraine as a mentally infirm drug user and a carrier of the AIDS virus who "may be responsible for the eventual deaths of numerous individuals. Her family and society bear some responsibility for what might have been."

"I answered that as a lawyer would and it still bothers me because I had to answer in a very vicious, legalistic way," he explained. "From what I had gathered that particular girl had been a former mental patient [and] had active HIV, so her life before she met me was not the most stable of lives. So for her family to get all of a sudden so excited about her death, [saying] we've been hurt to the sum of, I think it was five hundred fifty million dollars, I questioned it. Where were they before she got sick? Where were they after she got sick? She's still on the street. And now, the family woke up. [It's like] someone is suing you and you built the scaffold and you know you built it substandard, then you fall off the scaffold and sue the construction company for allowing you to be on the scaffold. You have some joint responsibility."

"How dare he?" I raged to myself, tempted to lunge across the table. Only after I remembered how critical I had been of Geraldo Rivera's response did I regain my composure. Joel was quick to blame Orvieto's parents for their daughter's transgressions so I asked him if his parents should shoulder some of the blame for the way he turned out. This time his explanation was not so glib. "They took me to a child psychologist. I went to the school psychiatrist, I went to a psychiatrist in my later teens," he said. "I happen to fall in one of those borderline areas where it's not really clear, so they missed it. But yes, there was an attempt by my parents to say 'hey, he's not functioning too well.' "

In early January 1992, Joel picked up Mary Ann Holloman, who sewed personalized G-strings for the exotic dancers at Goldfingers, an upscale Manhattan strip club that Joel could never afford on the East 12th Street stroll. He remembers the approximate date because it was within a few days of his father's birthday, which was January 5. At thirty-nine, Holloman would not only be Joel's oldest victim, she would also be one of the most formidable. "We ended up in the same parking lot as the Korean girl. In the middle of the [oral] sex act, I grabbed her throat. Very automatic. I just grabbed her and I got hit in the face, scratched, mauled. She was one of the ones who fought the most. Again, back to the work yard, park [the truck], [body] into [a] drum, [then dumped] into Coney Island Creek. Not much with that one."

Once again I was enraged at Joel's smugness. Perhaps it was because I now had a daughter of my own, but I started finding it increasingly difficult to put up with his callousness. The way he casually dismissed the dumping of Holloman's body was incomprehensible. He described it as if he were a fisherman hurling an undersized flounder back into the water.

Joel was always on the lookout for new strolls but he was by nature a creature of habit; it was astounding that his pickup truck never aroused the suspicions of either the prostitutes or the pimps. How could they not have taken notice that so many of their colleagues entered the truck and never returned? And what about the parasitic pimps? Weren't they supposed to be protecting these girls from creeps like Joel? With so many girls disappearing, why weren't they jotting down license plate numbers or at the very least making a mental note of the vehicles the girls entered? Even if they didn't truly care about their employees' physical well-being, wouldn't they at least be protecting their own investment?

"[The] Allen and Forsythe and First and Second [Avenue strolls] I had been going to maybe a hundred times," explained Joel. "I knew the area as much as I could know any area. So I knew most of the girls were independents. They had girl friends, but it wasn't a real pimp area. Where if you went to the [Jacob] Javits area, in those days it was right out of TV. The girls dressed the way the TV pros did, with the high plastic boots and fishnet, the feathers in their hair. And the pimp mobiles, with all the chrome and metallic paint. It was like 'Whoa,' let's advertise what we are doing here."

While Joel found the Javits action appealing, it was usually well beyond his price range. On the rare occasion when he could afford a girl there, he used his imagination to view the encounter as a conventional date. "I would go through the area like window shopping," he said. "Picked a couple of those girls up though. Generally that was fifty dollars and if you want to go to a hotel room it [was] a hundred for [the girl], plus [more money for] the hotel. Where at Forsythe and Allen you could get anything from around ten dollars up to forty, maybe fifty, depending on the drug of choice and how cheap it was and how clean she was. They were out every night. I don't care if it was fifty below or raining sheets. [But] they were generally lousy dates because [the sex was like] a machine on automatic."

Even by Joel's bloody standards, 1992 was a particularly violent year. Looking back, there are several factors that may have contributed to what he calls his "accelerated period." Not long after killing Holloman he picked up a girl he had admired from afar for quite some time but had never dated. Categorizing her as a "pro's pro," he wound up getting outfoxed at his own game. "She [was] a lot slicker than the other girls in that you have to drive past her a lot before you actually realize she's working," he explained. "She blends in a lot. Half the time I couldn't recognize her. She [had] this very fresh look about her, like she is not working. And her story is she works for call-girl agencies or brothels or occasionally on the street when she needs extra money. That is her story."

Once the woman got into Joel's truck he attempted to strangle her as he straddled her during oral sex. But she managed to turn the tables on him in a hurry. "She got her knee up and, extending her knees to her ankle, basically jacked me up like a car," he explained. "And I was on the roof of the truck. It broke contact because I was way up there, and your arms are only so long. When she put me down, we didn't get into a physical fight. She said something [like], 'You know you could hurt some of the smaller girls. We're not your girlfriend, we're not here to fool around, we're here to just do a job and get it over with.' And I drove her home, or what she called home."

As perturbed as he was with himself over that failure, things got worse when he went to a free clinic soon afterward for a blood test. His passivity regarding STDs turned to panic when he tested positive for hepatitis and several other blood disorders. Even though the city was gripped by an AIDS epidemic, Joel still seemed to think he was immune from that disease because he was not on the receiving end of anal sex. He had convinced himself it was nearly impossible to get AIDS from having conventional unprotected sex even with an HIV-infected woman. He had completely blocked out the possibility of contracting AIDS and would occasionally engage in oral sex, or even intercourse, without a condom. Hepatitis actually frightened him more than AIDS did, because in his mind, there was a much more realistic chance he might get it. This time it was a false alarm.

"I was Joe Blow as far as [they] were concerned," he said of his visit to the clinic. "Like everything else in life, you get what you pay for. So this was a free clinic and they screwed up the test and I came up positive with surface antigens and hepatitis. So that was fun for a couple of years, [living] with the paranoia." Despite that close call, he still continued to practice unsafe sex with hookers.

I think that Joel, believing he had acquired a potentially fatal disease, embarked on more frenzied murderous activity. By the end of 1992, he had claimed at least seven victims. On Mother's Day weekend he picked up Iris Sanchez, twenty-five, in his mother's car on the First Avenue stroll. He remembers the date because he was supposed to be working at his part-time job at an East Meadow liquor store, but blew it off when he became entwined in Sanchez's particularly gruesome murder. It takes Joel a few seconds to conjure up the images of her death, but he then brings it to life in sickeningly clinical detail.

"Picked her up in daytime," he remembered almost exuberantly, as if pleased at his ability to retrieve simple information. "We went to a housing project, by a tall building, not too far from the water [in downtown Manhattan], down by where Macy's has the fireworks."

After parking in the truck, their encounter was put on hold. "Where we parked it was quiet, [but] this guy shows up on a bicycle and starts scavenging in the Dumpster," Joel said. "So we waited for him to leave."

With no prodding whatsoever, Joel answered the next question before it was even asked. "In the back seat of Mom's car," he said.

"After sex?" I queried.

"During," he answered bluntly.

Although Joel steadfastly maintains he never had sex with the dead bodies of any of his victims, his answer to the following question raises doubt. "After you would do this [kill] during your sexual act, would you finish and have your orgasm?" I asked.

"Sometimes, sometimes not."

"So there were times when you finished with a dead body?" I probed further.

"No!" he exclaimed as if caught in a trap he should have seen coming. "I would have come during the strangulation."

In the forcefulness of his response, he implied that I had confused his words as much as some of the psychiatrists had in the past. I could not help being struck again by the twisted logic of this conversation. Joel had no trouble admitting he was one of the most savage killers in the annals of criminal lore, but how dare someone suggest he was a necrophiliac.

JOEL TOOK A CASUAL DRIVE BACK HOME to Long Island with the body of Iris Sanchez by his side, still uncertain about what he was going to do with the corpse. He drove his mother's Toyota across the Brooklyn Bridge, then headed east on Atlantic Avenue for about twenty miles. As he left Brooklyn and entered Queens, he reached an area he described as the the back end of Kennedy Airport.

"There is a waterway and a vacant lot, a big, long lot," he recalled. "There is a strip mall on one side and a vacant lot on the other side. And I saw some guys fishing and their cars were in there. So I just bopped right up the highway into the lot with Mom's car. There was like a six-inch curb. Crunched [the car]. Drove in there, found a mattress, dumped her under the mattress. Got home

Joel and I met while covering a boxing match between Rocky Fratto (left) and Steve Michaelerya for a national boxing magazine in 1979. I was the writer and Joel was the photographer. Boxing is known for being a particularly tough sport to shoot but Joel excelled at it. (*Joel Rifkin*)

Throughout our young lives Joel and I both had trouble harnessing our aggressions in appropriate ways. Unlike Joel, I found a healthy outlet by becoming a professional boxer. Although I have just landed a right hand to the face of Christian McCrudden (left) in this November 1982 matchup, I ultimately lost the fight. (*Collection of the author*)

Joel is escorted into a state police vehicle after being charged with the murder of Tiffany Bresciani. He later confessed to killing her "when things got out of hand" and also told investigators about the sixteen other women he killed during a four-year spree. (© *1993 Newsday, Inc. Reprinted with permission.*)

Although Joel claimed that he began to feel some degree of remorse for his actions when he observed the victims' family members during court proceedings, he doesn't appear to have a care in the world during this testimony. His attorney would blame his inability to stay awake on the nitrates in the bologna sandwiches he was served in jail. (© 1994 Newsday, Inc. Reprinted with permission.)

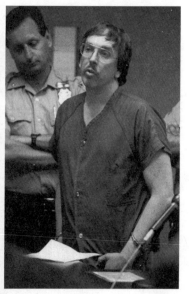

Joel angrily tells Suffolk County Judge John J.J. Jones that his constitutional rights have been violated on the day he is sentenced to a minimum of fifty years for the murders of Leah Evans and Lauren Marquez. He had hoped to get a delay in sentencing because of pain from a cyst that had recently been removed from his back. (© 1995 Newsday, Inc. Reprinted with permission.)

Former detective Ray Pierce, the NYPD's FBI-trained criminal profiler, believes that Joel's killing resulted from a sense of entitlement that formed after the years of abuse he had endured at the hands of others. (*Courtesy of Ray Pierce*)

Former NYPD sergeant Joe Piraino, an expert on serial killing, believes that once Joel committed his first murder, he had essentially "hatched" and there was no stopping him. (*Collection of the author*)

As I attempt to "demonstrate" the way in which Joel choked his victims, the most notorious killer in New York State history seems completely unmoved by our topic of conversation. (*Teddy B. Blackburn*)

Joel ponders some tough questions during a visit at the Attica Correctional Facility in the fall of 1999. *(Teddy B. Blackburn)*

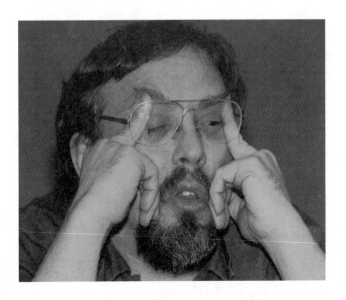

Joel's artwork is a study in contradictions. They range from biker chicks and grizzled football players to adorable animal portraits, most of which show bigger animals acting as protectors of smaller, more vulnerable ones. (*Collection of the author*)

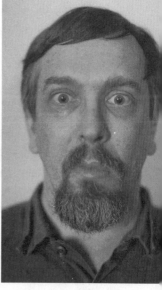

Left: If not for the prison uniform—and the ID number he'd been branded with for the rest of his life—Joel would look like a pleasant, unassuming fellow. *(Collection of the author)*

However, the photo at right shows a far different face, perhaps the one his scores of victims saw as he brutally took their lives. *(Chris Buck)* around eleven [in the morning]. Mom comes out of the house screaming at me, 'Where the hell have you been? Your boss called like three times.'"

Because it was Mother's Day weekend, business was brisk at the liquor store where Joel worked part time and he had been desperately needed. "We had a line out the back door of people buying stuff for dinner and the holiday and that kind of stuff," he said. "We had only two floor walkers at that time, and I was one of them. So he [the owner] was pretty pissed."

As exhausted as he was, Joel showed up at noon and worked until the store closed at nine. "He just yelled at me a lot, but didn't fire me," said Joel, who by now was displaying flair for living simultaneously on the edge of two opposite worlds. He was so adept at it, he carried Sanchez's ring, watch, and bracelet in his pants pockets for his entire shift. Despite being surrounded by mothers and families all day long, he never considered that Sanchez might have been a mother herself, or that she might have actually wanted to get home to her children that day. When Joel led NYPD and Port Authority detectives to her remains after his arrest fourteen months later, the skeletal body was still frighteningly adorned with one sock and a dress with large polka dots.

Joel uses the death of Sanchez and several of his other victims as twisted examples of why he had never become, in his mind at least, an expert killer. The way he sees it, he was nothing more than a confused, temporarily insane man who struck when the urge hit him, ramifications be damned. With Sanchez he managed to secure the carotid artery in his death grip and she was dead within ten seconds.

Even after all this time, Joel continues to underrate his proficiency as a killer. Never, he insists, did he grow completely confident or comfortable as a murderer. "I tried to explain [this] to one of the psychiatrists, [but] he missed what I was trying to say," he explained as he launched into one of his frequent athletic analogies. "I knew from my experience from the sports teams in high school that the more you practice something the more proficient you get at it. Basically, an athlete practices and gets better. That's the whole point of an athlete practicing. So if I had athletic ability progressing from [number] one, I should have gotten more adept at it. And I didn't."

He then cites the murder of Sanchez to prove his point. "If this was essentially a quick, fast kill, shouldn't the other ones have been the same way? Wouldn't the skill factor have increased? It hadn't. There is a form of strangulation involving the blood flow, not the air flow. The blood flow one is what they teach in the military, and it's supposed to be extremely quick. That is [what] I might have done with [Sanchez], but I was never able to repeat it."

Joel, who is implying that Sanchez was killed so efficiently by accident, is speaking of the carotid artery in the neck which, if squeezed, instantaneously cuts off the flow of blood to the brain. The victim is rendered unconscious immediately and dead shortly thereafter. "I didn't know about it then," he said. "But through doing things repeatedly, you should vary. Every athlete varies technique until they get better. I read [that champion golfer] Tiger [Woods] went into a slump, I think two years ago, where his swing was a little off. So he went back at it and did it and did it. Now he's won three major [tournaments] in a row and some ridiculous amount of [money]. So you learn from repetition and repetition, and I didn't. It never got to the point where I could automatically dispatch. You know, you see the commando movies or spy movies, you know, James Bond knows the technique, bang, that's it, the guy's out."

I could not believe what I was hearing. It seemed that Joel had deluded himself into believing he was not an expert killer and was somehow deriving power from that belief. And I felt that just by acknowledging these carefully constructed comments, which exonerated him from any responsibility for the deaths of these women, I was an accomplice. Joel had devised a unique method of compartmentalization, and I was certain he did not see himself as a cold-blooded killer—just some poor slob who became a murderer by happenstance. I had seen unique walls of defense in the past, but this one was beyond anything I could have ever imagined. Joel truly believed the lies he told himself, even as he compared his killing to some type of fantasy game or sporting event.

Asked if this was the period in his life when he felt most alive, Joel was a bit more analytical. "It's not about [being] alive, but [being] aware," he responded. "[Was there a] heightened sense of smell, color, feeling? Yeah, you go through that. Again, going to sports, an athlete remembers the great touchdown, that great home run. They can even remember it in slow motion. Even a guy like [Mark] McGwire who hits seventy [home runs] in a year, he'll remember one or two of them as being, you know, the ultimate home run. He can tell those stories in his eighties. Yeah, it's heightened sense. It's just not your everyday thing."

Just weeks later, Joel met and killed thirty-three-year-old Anna Lopez. Although her body would not be found for months, Anna's long-suffering mother, Maria Alonso, knew something was wrong right away. Her daughter had become addicted to crack six years earlier and was often away from home for months on end. But when she did not show up to retrieve her monthly Social Security check, Maria was certain something terrible had occurred. All of her fears came true when it was determined that her daughter had been killed on May 25th, just nine days before her regularly scheduled visit to pick up her check.

Although she had never displayed a great deal of confidence, Anna had been a somewhat happy child right up until her adolescence. But at the age of thirteen she tried to commit suicide by taking large quantities of the medication she had been given because of exposure to tuberculosis. The suicide attempt followed an incident in which she was slapped by her sister in front of a friend for not doing her share of household chores. After going into convulsions, she was admitted to Kings County Hospital, where electrical paddles were placed on her chest to shock her back to life. After her daughter's murder Maria could not get over the fact that her daughter had in essence died twice in one lifetime.

After being released from the hospital, despite receiving repeated warnings from the doctors about how serious the aftereffects of convulsions could be, Anna adamantly refused to attend follow-up appointments. Looking back, her mother thinks she may have suffered brain damage, which eventually led her on the road to ruin and the fateful meeting with the man who would take her once promising life.

At the age of twenty Anna had married a man with a serious drug problem. By the time their daughter was born not long afterward, Anna too was immersed in the drug culture. When her husband was imprisoned for a firearms conviction, she dutifully went to work in a sweater factory and wrote him every day. He died shortly after being released from jail, leaving his devastated wife alone with their four-year-old daughter. She soon had two more children by two different men, and began living solely for drugs.

At first Joel could not remember where he met her, but after focusing for a few seconds he broke into a grin, as if he were a child who had fetched a ball and now wanted a reward. "Okay, I got it, Atlantic Avenue, closer to Queens," he answered triumphantly.

They drove down a residential street that ended at the gates to a factory and Joel, once again, strangled another victim. With the now lifeless Lopez sprawled on his front seat, Joel drove north, stopping for gas somewhere between the Bronx and upstate Putnam County. As night turned into day, he found a dump near what he called "a forty-foot buffer zone of trees before the houses started," not far from the Park-N-Ride off Interstate 84 in Brewster. When Anna was found by a man who stopped to urinate in the woods less than a week later, an earring was discovered in her sweater, which she was still wearing. The other earring was recovered in Joel's room after his arrest, and would be the first established link to her.

"Her, I didn't intentionally keep anything, but an earring fell off that ended up in the truck," he recalled. The earring would not be the only thing left behind by this victim. Her spirit lived on as well, through the ceaseless efforts of her family to make sure that Joel paid dearly for her death and did not fall through the cracks in the legal system. The strength of their love, not the least bit diminished by Anna's addictions or reckless lifestyle, left a powerful impression on him. If Joel is to be believed, their actions enabled the smug and remorseless killer to at least publicly acknowledge some of the pain and suffering his actions had caused.

Within weeks Joel picked up twenty-one-year-old, sandy-haired Violet O'Neill in lower Manhattan. He took her home to East Meadow, then strangled and suffocated her after they had sex. He dismembered her body, then distributed it in the waters around Manhattan. Her torso was later found wrapped in black plastic in the Hudson River, her arms and legs in a suitcase.

By the end of the summer Joel was no longer able to handle the rigors of his landscaping business, so he packed it in and went to a temp agency to find work. In December the agency found him a job as a stock clerk at an Olympus Camera warehouse in Woodbury, Long Island. Joel was thrilled to be around cameras all day and, while it was only a temporary job, it was a full-time position that might have led to an actual career. The employee discount he was offered might have afforded him the opportunity to revisit his interest in photography had he not had a secret life. But, true to form, Joel was always a day late and a dollar short when it came to taking advantage of anything positive in his life. As usual, all of his money was spent before he even made it.

"[At] the two lower Manhattan strolls oral sex [was] around twenty [dollars] in the car," he explained. "Regular sex would be thirty. A hotel could be twenty. [I was earning] maybe a hundred twenty, a hundred eighty a week, depending if it was a four-day or five-day week, [or] if there was overtime. I knew there was a camera at [a] discount[ed] two hundred twenty-five I was trying to buy, which meant I would have had to put two paychecks together and I couldn't do it. In the year that I was there I couldn't put two paychecks together."

For a few weeks Joel tried desperately to use the Olympus job as a new beginning. But the lure of the streets proved to be too strong and the killing continued unabated. He began to view his deadly proclivity as just another in a long line of things he did not like about himself. "I don't think I'd be sitting in the retirement home in my eighties, [thinking] like I got away with this and that," he said. "There's no way. You can't get any lower. Well, I probably could have, but that's about as low as you can get."

Ray Pierce wholeheartedly disagrees with Joel's self-assessment. Even if Joel had gotten away with all his murders, Pierce believes he would never have been so reflective. "It would be a stretch to think Joel is capable of feeling anything for anybody other than himself," he said. "The fact is he is a classic psychopath, which makes him incapable of feeling anyone else's pain but his own. I am reminded of a ghoulish joke that clearly reflects just how a psychopath thinks. A serial killer is dragging a victim into the woods, all the while telling her what he is going to do to her. As she pleads for her life, he is delighting in the mental torture he is inflicting upon her. She tells him about her wonderful husband and children, aging and dependant parents, and all the great things she has to live for. He pays no attention to any of her pleas and instead says, 'How do you think I feel? After I kill you, I have to come out of these woods. By then it will be pitch black, and I'm afraid of the dark.'"

FROM LATE 1992 TO SHORTLY BEFORE HIS arrest in June 1993, Joel worked at Olympus with an old junior high school friend named Michael Brown. Because Joel's dilapidated vehicles broke down so often, it was not unusual for him to commute to work with his old pal. They would occasionally have lunch together at a nearby pizzeria and, although Joel rarely drank, sometimes went to Friday night happy hours with other employees at a local pub.

"We talked about work," Brown was quoted as saying in *New York* magazine. "That was about the extent of the conversation. There was nothing about his outside activities, nothing about what he did on weekends. He was the same as he had been in high school, a quiet person who kept a lot to himself. He didn't want to let people get to know him. He would ask what everybody else had done over the weekend, but when we asked him what he had done, it was always the same answer: 'Oh, nothing. I just hung out.'"

Brown remembered thinking it was odd that Joel never let anyone ride in either of his pickup trucks. "When we went out to lunch, we always took someone else's car or van," he explained. "He definitely didn't want anybody in the trucks. He didn't even want anybody to see them. Instead of parking with the rest of the cars, he would park off on the side, maybe four rows away where there were no other cars."

And clearly Joel had good reason for being so secretive. Right around the time Joel began working at Olympus and renewing his friendship with Brown, a municipal worker in Yorktown, an upscale northern Westchester suburb, made a gruesome discovery while relieving himself at the end of an empty cul-de-sac. The badly decomposed body of thirty-one-year-old Mary Catherine Williams was found lying in the snow amid a pile of branches. What was most haunting to the worker was her wide-open jaw, which looked as if it had let out a desperate shriek as it gasped its last breath. She had been killed sometime in the fall.

The Charlotte, North Carolina, native had been her high school homecoming queen, as well as a cheerleader at the University of North Carolina. The daughter of a dentist, Williams, who was briefly married to a football star back home, had always been an overachiever until moving to New York in 1987 to pursue an acting career. Her fairytale life came to an abrupt end when she quickly fell in with a bad crowd and became addicted to drugs.

A graduation photo of her shows a young woman with a deep, endearing, almost mystical smile. She looks like the perfect daughter, a loyal confidante, a trusted friend. By looking at the photo alone, one would be hard pressed to imagine her living and working on the streets of Manhattan.

"I had been with her two times before," said Joel. "She was a cheerleader. [Detectives] showed me wedding pictures, they showed me modeling pictures, a clip from a movie. They told me a lot of her history. I know she was a cheerleader down in North Carolina, she cheered on one of the squads that [James] Worthy and [Michael] Jordan played on, I guess when they took the national championship. [But] she was really strung out when I knew her. The streets just really thinned her out. Her nose looked different, her eyes [looked different]."

Joel said he had "a great time" with her the first time they dated, but was put off the second time around. "I picked her up and I basically dropped her off," he recalled. "She needed to get rubbers or something from a bodega and I pulled off. The next day I went down the same street at almost the same time and she is leaning on the same car, dressed the same way. I picked her up [and] we went to a small parking lot uptown, in the fifties [or] sixties."

Joel was once again driving his mother's Toyota, which became severely damaged in the ensuing fracas. "The neat thing about that was, Mom's car [had the] front seat with the bucket at full back," he said almost nostalgically. "She somehow bent the gear shift levers on the floor. It is an automatic, not a clutch [or] stick, it is a T in the floor. And she ended up bending it. And [after killing her], I almost couldn't get the car into drive."

Joel's description of the incident supports Joe Piraino's theory that he is incapable of empathy or of mustering up any degree of feeling for his victims. "I believe that Joel's actions were more about control than emotion," said Piraino. "He was able to perpetrate the act of killing with no emotion whatsoever. There was no rage, no elation, no intoxication during or after the act. All of his actions fed into his fetish for sexual sadism. The moment of the victims' capture is what got him excited. His actions were about the supreme power he felt over his own life and the destiny of his victims. He didn't love or hate them. It didn't matter if they were nice to him or not prior to the killing. That had no determination in the end result.

"Relationships for people like Joel are bound by fantasy, not reality," he continued. "His sexual world had no romantic spectrum. Most people have a capacity to know what is real and what is not. I think he was incapable of that differentiation. He knew what he was doing was wrong, but could not help but act on his impulses. He finally found some form of consistency in his life. The outcome was always the same. It didn't matter if it was evil, all that mattered was that the outcome was predictable. In a biblical sense Rifkin became a prophet. He could predict and control his victims' destiny. What power! Some people's reality is the soap operas they watch every day. To others the Andy Sipowicz character on [the television show] *NYPD Blue* is as real as it gets. For Joel it was killing, then mutilating scores of women. When he says he did that with no great display of emotion I am certain he is telling the truth."

While Joel always talks emotionlessly about the actual killings, he does display emotion when conveying extraneous bits of information related to the murder itself, more often than not when they could easily have resulted in his capture. Asked if he was ever elated or thrilled at any point during the actual crimes he flatly and very believably said no. "I was calm the whole period," he insisted. "There was sometimes, through outside cirumstances, that the excitement got a little [heavy]. One time the car wouldn't start. So I was almost stuck there with the body. I'm sitting there with a dead body at a crime scene and the car is not starting. That was, of all numbers, the thirteenth. All my phobias and stuff like that, [it seemed odd that with the] thirteenth body and the car's not starting."

Once he did get the car going, Joel said, he was anxious to get rid of the body but oddly drove sixty miles in the opposite direction of his home to do so. "She went to Yorktown the same night," he said, as if adding a sense of romanticism to his daring escape from danger. "It was maybe eight o'clock in the morning when I dumped her. I guess they [were] building an industrial park there but they only had two buildings built. So there is this long road that turns into this big circle for the semis to turn around in. And I accidentally found this road, went down there, and on the side of the semicircle parked and dragged her into the woods."

When authorities recovered Williams's property in Joel's room, they initially feared there were actually dozens, perhaps even hundreds, of additional victims. "She had this wicker-like picnic basket type suitcase full of costume jewelry," he explained. "There had to be a couple of hundred pieces of costume jewelry. And that got the state police excited because they thought it represented hundreds of girls."

After killing Williams, Joel was still vowing to himself that he would stop the madness. He tried on several occasions to get phone numbers from the girls so he could arrange indoor dates with them in advance. Joel theorized he would be doing the girls a favor by keeping them off the streets. Not only would another person probably be on the premises for their protection, he would also be able to get serviced in a casual, more laid-back location. But those plans went awry. "Some would give phone numbers and you would check the phone out, which I did once, [and] I got a Martin Paint store," he said. "Some want regulars, some don't. Some feel safer with regulars because they are off the stroll. They work out of their book [because they don't want to give their number to someone new or without references]."

Unfortunately for Joel, he was never willing or able to pay enough to make it into someone's book. Junkies, after all, don't usually work by appointment. But he was desperate to have some romance in his life, even if he had to pay for it, and was eager to have it away from the chaos of the streets. "There was more time involved, it was more absorbing," he explained. "You had to get to the room and you undress and you're talking, and you get dressed and clean up. That type of thing. The car can be five minutes, real quick."

Even though the number of Joel's victims was now well into the double digits, he knew he was tempting fate if he continued. There were too many close calls to ignore and it seemed clear he would soon be caught if he did not at least take a brief hiatus. Deciding who lived and who died was constantly tugging on his mind, often taking the sexual pleasure out of his encounters. Once he made that decision, the power of his undeniable impulse took over and he never knew when the urge would strike. In almost every instance, he remembers a calm before the storm. "If you go across the thirty-five years that I was a citizen, before I became an inmate, except for a brief spree of shoplifting [and] traffic tickets, that [murder] was about [the only crime I ever committed]," he said. "So it's really a small percentage of my daily life, an anomaly to my daily life. There was no trans-morphing into a werewolf or anything like that, like the psychs and the prosecutors want to portray. To use a cliché, [picking my victims] was like a bolt of lightning or whatever. It was that element. I mean just random choice. It could have been any of ten girls on a street corner. [I would make] resolutions with the full intention of, yeah, this is my last cigarette or I'm gonna exercise every day. And you exercise for about two weeks, three weeks, and stop. You find an excuse and you start again for one or two more days. It was very hard to control."

This is where Joel's definition of premeditation differs from most others. Asked if he ever said to himself, "tonight I'm going to go out and kill, not just have sex," he seemed genuinely baffled. "Yes and no," he responded. "There were times when I thought that would happen and it didn't happen. There were times where I had that idea and it did happen. But I don't know if it was a premeditated type thing. I think it was part of the fantasy and they overlapped. I think the homicides were more related to opportunity. There was one girl who was one of the few I was a regular with, and she became the face in all of the fantasy dreams. One night I picked her up and I was totally jazzed to do this, she was going to die that night. And I went to a spot that was very secluded. Everything was manipulated and set up to where, yeah, this could happen. And it didn't. We just had sex and I drove her back."

Jenny Soto was not so lucky. Joel picked up the slight twenty-three-year-old Latina on a stroll near the Williamsburg Bridge. One of three children, she never knew her father, who had been stabbed to death in a subway station a few months before she was born. The case has never been solved.

Raised by her mother, Margarita Gonzalez, and stepfather, a shipyard worker, in what is now the fashionable Park Slope section of Brooklyn, she dropped out of high school after the eleventh grade. Although she became a victim of the streets and was arrested several times for prostitution, Soto still had no shortage of goals that she was determined to bring to fruition.

Eager to become a dancer or model, she regularly bought film and had friends take photos of her, presumably to mail to agents. When her long-time boyfriend was imprisoned in January 1992, Soto met and fell in love with a rap singer named Popcorn who, at nineteen, was three years her junior. Popcorn was as serious as Soto was reckless, and a slow, positive change started coming over her. She talked about going back to school and even began canvassing music clubs to convince owners to audition Popcorn's group. She never missed one of his rehearsals and, much to her mother's delight, finally seemed to have her life back on track.

But no matter how hard she tried, Soto could not completely shake her drug habit. Around Thanksgiving 1992, she said goodbye to her sister at a downtown Manhattan subway station and is believed to have gone in search of drugs. She called her mother shortly before midnight to make sure her sister got home all right. It was the last time her mother ever heard her voice. When Joel solicited her on the corner of Allen and Eldridge Streets, she readily jumped into his pickup truck. After engaging in sex with her bespectacled customer, she found herself in the grip of Joel's bare hands. As slight as she was, Soto did not die passively and Joel later described her as "the toughest one to kill." She kicked and scratched, digging her nails into his face and neck as she desperately tried to escape. By the time Joel was finally able to break her neck, all of her fingernails had been broken in the struggle. After making certain she was dead, he removed her panties, bra, gold drop earrings, ID card, and syringe, then drove into the South Bronx where he dumped her body off a rocky hill and watched it land on the edge of the Harlem River, not far from where he deposited Yun Lee. A few days later it was found at Lincoln Avenue and 132nd Street; a huge billboard for Newport cigarettes flashed in the background. Soto was identified through her fingerprints, which were on file because of her numerous arrests.

Since many of Joel's victims had histories of disappearing without notice, most were not even reported missing. There was no evidence to even suggest a serial killer was on the loose. So when Soto's body was found the initial suspicion fell on her recently paroled ex-boyfriend. At the wake, where she was dressed in a turtleneck to hide the ghastly marks on her neck, the ex-boyfriend wept uncontrollably and unabashedly, while continually kissing her hands and face. Soto's mother was aghast at what she imagined to be his phony display of grief, and let him know in no uncertain terms that she believed he murdered her daughter. She pushed him away from the coffin, called him a killer, and swore to him that justice would eventually be served.

Joel still doesn't know why what he calls "the acceleration period" ended after the Soto homicide. He took a holiday hiatus, then resumed his killing in earnest soon after the new year. While trolling one night he picked up Leah Evans as she stood against a wrought iron fence on the First Avenue stroll. Evans was the twenty-eight-year-old daughter of a onetime Manhattan Civil Court judge. While police said she had lived an unconventional life, Leah Evans had no record of prostitution or drug arrests. She lived in Park Slope with her mother, a public relations woman, and her two children, a boy, four, and a girl, two. After spending two years at Sarah Lawrence College in Bronxville, the only employment she was able to find was as a waitress and a cook.

"She may not have been a regular working girl," said Joel. "She may have gotten mugged or robbed earlier in the day. She had a regular job and I guess needed money that night. After we got to the parking lot and got half undressed, we were getting ready, she decides 'no, no, let's not do it here, let's go to a girlfriend's house.' A lot of times I had done that with other girls in the street and usually got ripped off. So I decided to stay there, [even though] she was uncomfortable. [She] started complaining, even crying, and [I] couldn't perform anyhow and I strangled her."

Joel drove Evans to the east end of Long Island, trying to put as much distance as possible between him and the scene of the crime. During the off season the east end is fairly uncrowded, so Joel had no trouble finding a deserted road. "I thought it was a service road, [but] it was a dirt road that just took a little turn out," he recalled. "I guess that it is where kids go to park, make out, or whatever, because there was an old campfire there. So I figured, okay, I'll take her into the woods in that area. It was nice and secluded. This was the only girl I buried; shallow grave, did like a sod cut. Took a square of undergrowth, vines and stuff straight up, and put it straight down."

As hard as he tried to make the body disappear, he failed miserably. Several months later, on May 9, a group of Asian nature lovers from Queens trekked to the area to hunt for edible ferns. Much to their horror, they stumbled upon Evans's hand, still adorned with red fingernail polish, sticking creepily out of the earth. The hand was attached to a body that was in an advanced state of decomposition. "I guess through rigor [mortis] or whatever, the hand came up through the soil," said Joel, who was not very proud of his work. "That was the only one that hit the paper that I was aware of."

As nervous as he usually was, Joel does not remember being overcome with fear at the discovery of the body. He figured he'd placed enough distance between his residence, the place of occurrence, and the location of the disposal to make him immune from suspicion. For almost two months police were unable to identify the gruesome find, and they had even arranged to have a computer-generated composite sketch of the victim made by a forensic anthropologist in Knoxville, Tennessee. That proved to be unnecessary when some of Evans's property was found in Joel's bedroom.

The next victim was Lauren Marquez, a twenty-eight-year-old Tennessee native who had been raised in a military family. The mother of two, Marquez loved her children dearly but was so addicted to drugs that her habit had consumed her life. By the time she arrived in New York all of her energies were geared toward staying high. Joel picked her up on the corner of East 11th Street and Second Avenue, near a Japanese restaurant. He had seen her many times before but had never chosen her as a date. "She was pretty tall, I had seen her on the street a lot," he recalled. "She was one of the girls I would go to talk to, but I never picked her up because she was just very played out. I mean scary played out. She was young, but very thin and tall. I don't think she could find a working vein in her arms. But she had an amazing face and amazing blue eyes. Almost gray-blue, you know, that silvery effect."

When she and Joel arrived at a location for sex Joel immediately grabbed her neck. "[But] I couldn't get the seal," he lamented. "And this is another one where my memory didn't match the reports that were generated. Because apparently she had a broken rib or two."

Told that perhaps the broken ribs came from an angry boyfriend, vengeful pimp, or even a past customer, Joel seemed uninterested. "Could be, but I don't know," he replied almost flippantly. "And she was dumped in Suffolk County."

It was only after Joel was arrested, confessed to her murder during intense questioning, and directed police to the body that Marquez was found in the Pine Barrens of eastern Long Island, not far from where Evans was deposited. "[It was in] one of the not-so-stylish Hamptons, near an Air Force field," he said. "There is a golf course, and across from the golf course there is an access road for LILCO [the Long Island Lighting Company] for the overhead lines. And I pulled up that dirt road and about a half a mile up that road I pulled over and dragged her into the woods." He was asked if he kept any trinkets that had been in her possession. "May have been a souvenir," he responded breezily. "I'm not sure."

It was during my second visit to Attica that Joel relayed these specifics of all seventeen of his murders. While he at first held my rapt attention and that of photographer Teddy B. Blackburn, by the time Joel was halfway through the chronology we were not only completely desensitized to what we were hearing, we were also downright bored. At one point I looked over at Teddy and saw that he was fast asleep. Intellectually I was troubled because it felt as if I was minimizing the value of the victims' lives by not listening intently to the grisly details of their deaths. But I was quickly brought back to reality by a startling revelation. It was the off-hand monotony of Joel's descriptions that had caused me to become uninterested and to experience, in essence, the same lack of emotion he lived with for so long. I still shudder at the thought that, temporarily, I had become as immune to savagery as he had been all along.

THE STRANGE CIRCUMSTANCES SUR-
rounding the recovery of Leah Evans's body, which
occurred after the murder of Lauren Marquez, resulted in a great deal of local media coverage.
Newsday, which is Long Island's only major re-
gional newspaper, and WLNY, the area's local television station, ran with the story for weeks. Joel
grew increasingly paranoid and began having intense premonitions about getting caught. Having
never handled stress effectively on any level, he
began to get more and more sloppy in every aspect
of his life. While many in the law enforcement
community believe this negligence proves he may
have subconsciously wanted to be captured, Joel
still maintains that was in no way accurate. But
his actions with the woman who would prove to be

his last victim were incredibly bizarre, and seem to support the authorities' claim.

While driving his mother's since-repaired Toyota along the Allen Street stroll on an early June morning, Joel spotted twenty-two-year-old Tiffany Bresciani. She was wearing a mid-length skirt and a sheer blouse that buttoned up the front. He could not help noticing her breasts, which were outlined against the blouse, as well as the purple rose tattoo that encircled her wrist. Enhancing his desire even more was the fact that he had seen her performing at an Eighth Avenue sex emporium called the Big Top Lounge just weeks earlier and had been transfixed. Although his level of sexual arousal was high, he still says he had no plan to kill her.

The normally savvy Bresciani, a native of Metairie, Louisiana, who had come to New York in the hope of being a dancer, was high on cocaine and methadone that night, and perhaps her judgment was impaired. But Joel was so nondescript, so ordinary looking, she must have thought he looked harmless. After she agreed to straight sex for a fee of twenty dollars, Joel took her to the New York *Post* parking lot. He had difficulty getting a sufficient erection, a problem that was compounded by the appearance of an interloper who, had he looked inside the car, could have borne witness to a murder in progress.

"We were getting ready for sex," Joel recalled.

"She was scrunched down and I was taking my pants off or whatever. [I'm] just about to start and a van parks next to us and a guy gets out and walks behind the car. I thought [he] walked off, so I grab the neck, strangle her, you know, she's struggling a little bit. We're doing whatever in the back seat of the car, and I look up just after she passes out, and the guy is standing three feet from the car doing Tai Chi. [He's] facing the water, watching the sunrise, [doing a] praying mantis [position], and all this other crazy stuff."

All of his premonitions notwithstanding, Joel had no way of knowing then that Bresciani would be his final victim or that he was enjoying what would amount to his last seventy-two hours of freedom. He still does not fully understand why he killed her in the first place. "Tiffany was [killed at] sunrise, five-thirty A.M.," recalled Joel. "And before her I was with a girl at around two. And the night before I was with two girls. And a couple of days prior to that I was with a girl. So why her and not the others? Certainly why not the girl at two o'clock? Why three hours later?

"If you want to talk about [my killing spree] in entirely illogic[al] scenes, that was it," he continued. "I killed Tiffany in the back seat, drove home [at] seven o'clock in the morning, she is in the back seat of the car, [the] bench seat, totally naked. There was this giant sink hole I knew [about where] I could have, like, slid her out of the car [near where she was killed]. But I didn't. I went home on the LIE [Long Island Expressway], which again is with the high trucks and buses. That wasn't bright either. And I drove around the neighborhood and I picked up a large patio window that I was going to use for a greenhouse. None of it makes any sense. There were other girls where the same night [they] were killed, [and] within an hour or two [they] were disposed of. This time none of it makes sense."

Once back in the relatively safe confines of his home, his behavior got even odder. "I went through the house literally, the kitchen, and out the front door, [telling my mother] 'I got to do something real quick, I'll be back, don't worry, yada-yada, yada-yada,' grabbed some more money, drove to Kmart," Joel said excitedly as if reliving the frenetic pace of the moment. "Girl is still in the back seat. I go in [to the store]. I bought anti-freeze, oil, and a tarp. Drove to another lot, girl is still in the back seat. [Wrapped] her in the tarp, transferred [the body] to the trunk. I come home. Mom has to borrow the car to do some shopping. It is her car, she is 'borrowing' her car back."

Joel was beside himself with worry when his mother took off to do her chores, oblivious of the fact that she was transporting around the corpse of a young woman that her son had killed just hours earlier. He knew that under normal circumstances his mother would never go in the trunk, but because of his premonitions he started thinking she'd probably get a flat tire or be struck from behind by another motorist.

"I [had] a little anxiety attack," Joel said jokingly, downplaying the intense terror he experienced on that fateful morning. "But [there was] nothing I could do about it. She comes back twenty minutes, a half hour later. I drove her to work that day, [then] drove home. Now there are only two vehicles at home that work: my truck, [the one] that runs, and her car. I have four and a half hours [until Mom comes home]. Instead of disposing of the body, I put the body in the garage, [then] take the truck that runs and disconnect the engine because I was going to switch the engine from one [truck] to another. [I] thoroughly dismissed [the fact] that I have this body."

Things got even worse as the day progressed and his date with destiny approached. His mother and sister, who had since moved back home, rarely went into the garage, mainly because it so closely resembled Joel's bedroom. It was knee deep and wall to wall with engine parts and gardening equipment, as well as useless machinery, hardware, and junk that Joel, always a compulsive collector and pack rat, had been accumulating at flea markets and from curbside trash heaps for ages. But on this day, Jan did try to make her way into the garage in search of an orange wheelbarrow that her mother needed for gardening. But as soon as she entered she was repelled by the intimidating amount of debris and her brother's stern admonition to stay out.

"You couldn't maneuver in the garage and I basically reminded my sister, 'What could you possibly be looking for, because you will never find it?' " Joel recalled. "And she made a pouty face, gave up, and went back inside."

While Joel insists that he had no deep-seated desire to get caught, his subsequent actions are quite perplexing. Perhaps he was overcome by mental and physical exhaustion, apathy, or just plain laziness. With a body to dispose of, why he chose to incapacitate both of his vehicles is anyone's guess. While it certainly could imply that he was either insane or determined to get caught, Joel says it was just another example of his inability to focus on several things at once. Once he decided to fix the truck his scattered personality made him incapable of focusing on anything else. "Now I'm focusing on this truck project," he said. "And for the next three and a half days, that is what I focused on. Just left her in the garage."

While several girls had been kept in the basement of the Rifkin household for days when Joel was home alone, and even more were stored at the rental lot, Bresciani was the only one ever placed in the garage of the family home. It did not matter to the killer that he shared that home with his mother and sister, either of whom could have found a thousand reasons to go into the garage, especially in the month of June when gardening is a major preoccupation on Long Island. Joel, who had not slept for several days by that point, claims that Bresciani was stored there only because he had become so preoccupied with his truck project and didn't have the energy to deal with disposing of the body.

But once she was killed, he claims he took no further liberties with her body and has no idea how she received the injuries investigators asked him about. "[The authorities] claim that Tiffany had injuries to her vulva area, [the] inside area beyond the vagina," he said. "News to me. And there's a few other incidents that [have been] related to me [about injuries incurred by the murder victims] that I have no idea [about]."

Joel believes his actions over the next few days are in no way indicative of a criminal mastermind but of a young man who was temporarily insane at the time. Leaving the body to ferment in the intense June heat, Joel's only concern was getting his truck running so he could dispose of the body. He had already earmarked an area by Republic Airport in Melville, about fifteen miles northeast of his home. Ironically enough, the one time Joel had an actual disposal plan it tripped him up and got him arrested. In hindsight, he realized that while Bresciani was doomed from the moment he picked her up, in effect so was his freedom.

He called the entire Bresciani episode a mess, saying it was out of control, because it occurred at the "wrong time of day, [with] people walking around. This was a total nightmare of nightmares," he said. "Being in a nightmare and having a nightmare at the same time. Like whatever could go wrong was going wrong."

It was about three o'clock in the morning on June 28, 1993, when state troopers Deborah Spaargaren and Sean Ruane spotted Joel's truck driving eastbound on the Southern State Parkway. He had left his home just minutes earlier after dabbing Noxzema under his nostrils to quell the stench of Bresciani's rotting corpse, which was now four days old. Although Joel was maintaining the fifty-five-mile-per-hour speed limit, the young officers, who were four hours into an uneventful shift, observed that his vehicle did not have a rear license plate. Joel, who was not carrying his driver's license or vehicle registration, cursed aloud when the officers flipped on their overhead lights so he would pull over. Knowing that the troopers would immediately smell the rancid odor of Bresciani's decaying body, he decided to make a run for it. At that point, he reasoned, he had nothing to lose.

When Joel refused to stop his vehicle Spaargaren grabbed the microphone of her public address system and sternly ordered him to do so. But Joel, who could feel and hear Bresciani's body rolling around in the bed of his truck, did not heed the order. He left the parkway at Exit 28 South, Wantagh Avenue, negotiating a sharp, horseshoe-shaped turn at an excessive rate of speed. He then bore through a stop sign, ignored a no-left-turn sign, and gunned the motor. The troopers, meanwhile, radioed for assistance and, before long, were joined by several other state police units, as well as mobile units from the Nassau County Police Department.

As frightened as he was, Joel was exhilarated by the chase, and soon had his truck up to ninety miles per hour as he roared past scores of slower-moving vehicles. Many oncoming autos were forced into a game of chicken with the desperate killer, but wisely turned their vehicles onto the shoulder of the road to avoid a collision. Realizing there were now countless vehicles behind him, Joel knew the jig was up. He had no choice but to go for broke. The only alternative was jail, which he knew in his gut could be a lifetime banishment. Making a silent, last-minute pact with himself, he decided he was either going to get away or he was going to die trying.

"If it wasn't her [Bresciani], it would have been the next one or the next one [that got me caught]," said Joel. "Eventually something would have hung me up and I would be here. We were talking about the practice and the skill and [how I should have been] getting better. I definitely did not get better. There was no learning curve."

He stepped on the gas, forcing the battered pickup to its limits. After speeding recklessly for twenty minutes through winding country roads lined with horse farms, commercial areas, and suburban housing tracts, Joel overshot Old Country Road, a main east-west thoroughfare. He lost control and the truck climbed a curb and flipped up onto two wheels. By some miracle it did not roll over and only came to rest after careening into a wooden utility pole not far from the county courthouse. The police officers skidded to a halt and ordered him out of the vehicle at gunpoint. Joel did not say a word as he submitted, and even voluntarily lay on his stomach and placed his hands behind his back. When Ruane informed him of the fact that he had no license plate on his truck, Joel was outraged at himself. The dead body had yet to be discovered, but Joel knew then and there that he alone had done himself in. He silently cursed himself for his own stupidity as Spaargaren snapped handcuffs on his wrists, just as she removed an orange-handled X-Acto knife from his back pocket.

14

"WHEN I WAS ARRESTED IT WAS A GREAT relief," Joel asserts to this day. "I remember sleeping on the floor as soon as the interrogation was over. I slept for a couple of days in the lockup."

Although Joel readily admitted killing Bresciani, saying "things got out of hand," he was not so quick to give up the other sixteen murders. Apart from his solicitation arrest, Joel had no experience with the criminal justice system and authorities expected him to be a lot more agitated and upset, especially since he was about to be charged with murder. Veteran state police investigators were troubled by the oddly composed demeanor of this man who had been caught red-handed driving around with the decomposing body of a woman he had already admitted to killing.

It would take hours for the floodgates to open, but once Joel started talking he could not, or would not, stop. It was one of the few times in his life when he had center stage, and he took full advantage of his rapt, almost deferential audience. While he displayed the same candor with me during my first Attica visit over seven years later, the medication he was on seemed to make him, on the surface at least, a lot less desperate for the attention he was clearly reveling in after his arrest. As much as he enjoyed the forum I provided him, he did not seem all that eager to please me.

But in 1993 it was obvious that he gained some satisfaction from his newfound notoriety. Attention, whether from teachers, contemporaries, colleagues, or, especially, women, had eluded him for as long as he could remember. Finally, in some bizarre way, he had made it. Not only were people of authority clinging to his every word, Joel had all the answers and, in his mind at least, he was the man in charge. Although he was in quite a legal predicament, the attention was like an intoxicant for him. He had dreamed and fantasized about being the center of attention since he was a small boy. Joel was finally feeling wanted, needed, and important. As strange as it sounds, he could not have enjoyed his interrogation more.

While he later claimed to have asked for an attorney on several different occasions and that his pleas were disregarded, his statements were ultimately ruled admissible. Many investigators believe there are other victims who died by Joel's hands that will probably never be discovered because, after thirteen hours of questioning, he did speak to a lawyer. The attorney immediately ordered the police to cease the interrogation. While Joel says that he had already chronicled all of the murders by this point, some investigators feel that, had he been allowed to keep talking, Joel would have told of other homicides. Before the interrogation was halted, Joel had even written in his own hand a list of where many of the bodies were dumped. The point at which Joel stopped talking leads me to believe he would have had more to say about his murderous activities.

As word of Joel's arrest spread, reporters descended upon his neighborhood and began talking with anybody who even remotely knew him, most of whom were shocked and flabbergasted. "It's all very strange," said Joy Reiter, who lived next door to the Rifkins for more than three decades. "They're very gentle people, they've been wonderful neighbors. They're very concerned citizens. The kids are sweet." Her equally shocked husband, Hal, could not have agreed more, saying, "He was a gentle, courteous kid."

"His family was so community minded," added Frances Parisi, who taught American history to

Joel in high school. "I never knew a more loving family."

Parisi had to be talking about Joel's parents, both of whom always seemed to be involed in some civic or social cause. The fact that most people considered Ben so gregarious and welcoming and Jeanne perfectly content at his side hints at the perpetual paternal shadow Joel inhabited throughout his life, even after his father had died. The comments by Frank Saracino, who had been acting principal at East Meadow High School when Joel was a student there, substantiated that. "Joel was not an aggressive person," he said. "If his father had not been on the board of education, I might not remember him at all."

"I don't believe it," asserted Alan Whitlock, a high school friend who had often spent time at Joel's house as a teenager listening to records by Led Zeppelin and the Eagles. "I'm sorry, even if I heard it from him I wouldn't believe it."

"[He] was just like any other kid," said Irving Adelman, the head of the public library's reference department where Joel had worked for several years after school. "It's not like a movie, where they look evil like in *Silence of the Lambs*, when you just know the first time you see him. He was just a normal kid."

As ordinary as he might have seemed to others at the time, there was really nothing ordinary about

Joel at all. Not only was he adopted, he was also dyslexic, uncoordinated, and mentally, emotionally, and physically tormented for the vast majority of his childhood. It's hard to imagine that, without receiving years of intensive therapy, anyone could emerge from such circumstances without some form of pathology. As vile and unforgivable as his crimes were, it is shocking how so many of his tormentors absolved themselves of any responsibility for his development. Some of them even seemed to be laughing at him now as much as they had then.

"He was a nerd," said one female high school classmate, as if that explained the entire psychopathology of serial killing. "His pants were too tight and he had white socks. He was geeky."

Once Joel's questioning ceased, he was transferred to the Nassau County Correctional Facility, which was located just blocks from his home on Carmen Avenue in East Meadow. Like its most notorious inmate at the time, the facility was a study in contrasts. Four decades before Joel's arrival there, the jail was surrounded by farmland and inmate trustees could regularly be seen working the fields through coils of barbed wire. But in the mid-fifties a man named Sam Levitt transformed the area into one big suburban housing development full of cookie-cutter homes. Urban dwellers looking to escape the oppressive conditions of the city came searching for suburban bliss in East Meadow. It didn't matter that their houses were within walking distance of the county lockup and they could not know they would be neighbors of a ticking time bomb named Joel Rifkin, an apparently awkward, fumbling, harmless boy next door.

Joel became known officially as CC 93005860, and his prison attire consisted of a two-piece orange cloth uniform. He was housed on the second floor in a dimly lit, windowless six-by-nine-foot jail cell that was reserved for only the most high-profile inmates. His particular cell was jokingly referred to by guards as "the conference room" because it had once been used as a meeting place for prisoners and lawyers. With guards watching his every move twenty-four hours a day, he crapped on a seatless toilet and washed in a cold aluminum basin. As exhausted as he was, the first thing he noticed was the striking contrast with his room back home. For the first time in his life he would be living free of clutter—from the mountains of junk he obsessively collected and from the mental and emotional clutter he'd accumulated while living in two divergent worlds. He didn't know that he would eventually view getting arrested as possibly the best thing that ever happened to him.

At the time, Joel was not so analytical. All he wanted to do was sleep, though the fact that he might be spending the rest of his life in state prison, or at the very least in a hospital for the criminally insane, did gnaw at him. Intellectually, he still had a natural inclination to be free, but the sense of relief was overwhelming. The relief was not because he would never kill again, but because he would no longer have to live with such a colossal secret. He instinctively knew that in prison his choices were few. Having made the wrong choices for his entire life, he was just glad that, for the time being at least, he wouldn't have to make any choices at all.

Seventeen days after being arrested and confessing to the murders of seventeen women, Joel, dressed in a rumpled striped shirt and gray pants and with his feet shackled, pled not guilty to killing Tiffany Bresciani. In attendance that day was Margie Gonzalez, the sister of Jenny Soto, as well as their mother, Margarita, and Maria Alonso, the mother of Anna Lopez. Converged upon by reporters eager for a scoop, Gonzalez gave them a perfect sound bite. "To me, he's an animal," she said.

Anna Lopez's family also began showing up at every court hearing, desperate to look the killer of their beloved Anna in the eye. They would prove to be a formidable presence. Fueled by an irrepressible anger, they spoke to the press in emotionally wrenching terms. They were determined to ensure that Joel did not get off through some obscure loophole. Their ubiquitous presence in Joel's little world finally made him realize, on some limited level, that he had not just been "blowing up tanks" or "shooting down planes."

"[The victims] stopped becoming objects toward the pretrial [stages] when I started seeing pictures and started hearing histories," he explained. "When I originally told the tale, it was number one, number two, right away it became 'this is Jane, this is Mary, this is Susan,' all of a sudden they had names. All of a sudden there were families outside the courtroom. That's when I began to realize they were not objects."

Attorney Robert Sale was the first of Joel's many lawyers. Known as a brilliant jurist, he devised a strategy to give his notorious client a remote shot at eventual freedom. Because Joel's confession had not been recorded or audiotaped, Sale knew there was the possibility it might get squashed altogether. If that didn't work, he would try to get all of Joel's murders, which fell under nine separate jurisdictions, tried under one roof in Nassau County. He theorized that Joel might be able to get a sympathetic jury from his home county to believe he was insane.

Sale argued that the taxpayers would save hundreds of thousands, perhaps millions, of dollars in court costs by consolidating the trials. But Fred Klein, a pit bull of an assistant district attorney who was no stranger to big cases, understood Sale's plan. He knew that if Sale, who had a history of moving mountains in a courtroom, could get just one juror to have reasonable doubt or could get Joel found guilty by reason of insanity none of the other jurisdictions would ever get a shot at him. Klein wisely decided to go forth on his own.

Joel, who was enjoying his time in the spotlight, began to grow envious of Sale's ability to manipulate the media. Having practiced law for nearly thirty years, the barrister had a sterling reputation that would have served the defendant well. But the killer's runaway ego made him more delusional by the day, and he began to see himself as an equally effective counselor. While he should have been thrilled to have such an esteemed lawyer working on his behalf, Joel decided, in what could have been the most compelling argument that he was indeed insane, to make a change. With a host of publicity-seeking lawyers visiting him daily, Joel terminated the services of Sale, even though Sale had already conferred with a host of forensic psychiatrists and set up a battery of tests that could have laid the groundwork for a successful insanity defense.

Joel still did not totally grasp how dire his situation was. He hired John Lawrence, for whom a friend of his had interned while a law student, and Michael Soshnick, a former Nassau County assistant district attorney. Soshnick had no real experience trying cases of a psychiatric nature but he had conducted many retention hearings while working as an ADA. They were held to determine whether defendants found guilty by reason of mental defect were dangerous or not and whether they should live in secure or non-secure facilities.

If Joel's narcissistic tendencies had surfaced in his relations with Sale, they became even more intense with his new counsel. By now a fixture in the jail's law library, he started to view himself as the choreographer of his own defense and fired off a letter to Lawrence and Soshnick that said: "Gentlemen . . . If I say something is important it is! . . . This trial is not to make either of you look good but to make me look good."

Joel's preliminary hearings, which would decide what evidence would be permissible at trial, kicked off in November 1993. If it was determined that his rights had been violated by not allowing him to contact an attorney before being questioned, then all of his subsequent statements would be suppressed. Joel was in his glory, relishing his imaginary role as the gatekeeper to his own defense. In the midst of the hearings the DA's office offered Joel a minimum sentence of forty-six years to a maximum of life imprisonment to satisfy all of the charges against him. The DA's office and Joel's legal representatives were amazed at his adamant refusal to accept such a generous plea bargain. Joel was banking on being guilty by reason of insanity or having his statements suppressed because of police and prosecutorial misconduct.

Joel assumed he would probably be found guilty of the Bresciani murder but foolishly believed he could walk on the other charges. After all, he reasoned, he could argue that except for his admission in Bresciani's murder, his admissions were moot because he had not been advised of his rights in a timely fashion. And even if he had, his mental condition precluded him from understanding them. He further believed that the plethora of evidence confiscated from his room had been obtained illegally because, even though the officers obtained a search warrant, they never told his mother what her son was being charged with. If they had she would have immediately retained the services of a lawyer, thereby ending the interrogation. The way Joel had things figured out he would serve twenty-five years or less for Bresciani's murder, then be released while still in his fifties to live his life as an eccentric celebrity writer. Having always viewed himself as a writer, he figured his criminal conviction would only add to his commercial appeal.

But a little over five months after his arrest, Joel's celebrity was eclipsed. On December 7, a thirty-five-year-old Jamaican-born man named

Colin Ferguson blasted his way onto the front pages of every newspaper in America by opening fire on scores of unsuspecting passengers on a Long Island Railroad evening commuter train. Standing in the aisle of the train, which was traveling from Penn Station to Garden City, he started spraying the car with bullets from a Ruger firearm. By the time the shooting stopped, six commuters were dead and more than twenty people, including a pregnant woman, were seriously injured.

Ferguson occupied the media spotlight for the next few months, while Joel found himself relegated to supporting player status. When they were finally housed together in an especially secure section of the county jail dubbed Murderers' Row, they got into a fistfight in a common area while awaiting transportation to court. Joel emerged the clear-cut loser, complete with shiner. He could not believe his misfortune. Even with a reputation as a particularly vicious and sadistic killer, Joel was still being picked on by the schoolyard bully.

Ferguson, a pudgy, soft middle-aged man, physically and emotionally overpowered Joel, a much bigger, stouter fellow who had snuffed out the lives of nearly three times the number of victims. Where was the justice? What did Joel have to do to command some small amount of respect in his new social circle? Even behind bars, he was seen as the same loser he had been for much of his life.

Thanks to Ferguson, Joel's one-man show quickly lost its luster. Only a few diehard media types stayed on the Rifkin case throughout the hearings, which often took place without a television camera in sight. From a media perspective Ferguson's case was a much bigger story. After all, his victims were professional people heading home to the safety of the suburbs after a long day at work. Unfair as it was, when compared with Ferguson's victims Joel's victims were far less attractive. Many people viewed them as the dregs of society, while Ferguson's victims represented the quintessential American middle and upper-middle class. They were a lot easier to relate to than the motley group of drug-addicted prostitutes who had tragically crossed Joel's treacherous path.

The surprise defense witness at Joel's pretrial hearing was Dr. Naftali Berrill, an esteemed psychologist who had interviewed Joel for ten hours. Besides possessing a doctorate in clinical psychology from Vanderbilt University, he was a faculty member at both the John Jay College of Criminal Justice in Manhattan and Adelphi University on Long Island. He had done postdoctoral work in neurophysiology, was a lecturer on antisocial personality disorder, and was the director of the New York Forensic Mental Health Group. If anyone could talk Joel out of a lifetime in prison, this man seemed the most qualified.

Dr. Berrill said Joel had a bipolar disorder, suffered from major depression, and was hypomanic (frenzied and out of control) during his four-year killing spree. More important, by virtue of the fact that Joel had been awake for at least three days at the time of his arrest and had spent most of that time greatly distressed about the body in the garage, Berrill believed that Joel was incapable of understanding the Miranda warnings, if, in fact, they had even been read to him. The claim that Joel was distressed about the body is in direct contrast to what he told me years later, when he said his entire focus turned to switching engines in his truck.

When Berrill's arguments failed to work in Joel's favor, the deflated defendant attempted to fire Soshnick on the spot, but the lawyer convinced him that making such an important decision on his own might imply to others that he was in fact sane. Joel kept the lawyers on but continued to make flippant suggestions regarding his defense. He also demanded that they secure movie and television rights to help pay for his legal fees. This contradicts Joel's later contention to me that the family of Lorraine Orvieto was trying to garnish any future monies he might generate by filing the wrongful death lawsuit against him. Joel implied that they were idiots for not knowing that New York's Son of Sam law precluded him from making any money from his crimes or subsequent incarceration. That being the case, he should have known that he could not profit from movie or television rights.

It was starting to look as if the only idiot in the courtroom was a nefarious killer with an above-average IQ who was trying desperately to masquerade as a lawyer. As laughable as that seems, Joel's sense of importance became even more inflated in the years to come.

15

JOAN MAHER* WAS JUST A FEW YEARS younger than Joel and had grown up in a neighboring town. After high school she studied elementary education at a local college and was eagerly looking forward to becoming a teacher one day. A serious young woman, Maher was a voracious reader who devoured and relished true crime sagas. Having read quite a bit about Ted Bundy, she was both disgusted and mesmerized by his horrific actions. But Maher was able to keep the kind of emotional distance between herself and the victims that a reporter or police officer would.

Maher's objectivity was tested when she was called for jury duty in the spring of 1994. Although

*Pseudonym.

she was not ultimately picked as a Rifkin juror, she is able to offer a compelling account of the selection process. Prosecutors had amassed a jury pool of over one thousand people but were having a tough time finding anyone not predisposed to finding Joel guilty even before going through the formality of a trial. With the trial looming the case was once again garnering widespread media coverage, so Maher, who knew from the beginning she could not be impartial, was initially relieved when she was ordered to report to civil court instead of criminal court. But because she had no shortage of morbid curiosity about the Rifkin case, that relief soon turned to disappointment.

Maher, who was then working as an assistant bank manager, dutifully reported to the courthouse along with several hundred other potential jurors. There were rumors throughout the day that they were going to be bused over to criminal court for consideration as jurors in the Rifkin proceedings. The first question potential jurors were being asked by both prosecutors and defense attorneys was whether they could be unbiased in such a bloodcurdling, emotionally charged case. Hundreds of people per day were disqualified when they responded that they could not.

Although New York State had no death penalty at the time, many people assumed it was in effect, especially for crimes as ghastly as serial murder.

Perhaps some of the jurors were afraid they might have to send Joel to his death after convicting him, something they would find difficult to live with. In actuality, the maximum sentence available for one murder, which was all Joel was being tried for at the time, was twenty-five years to life. That meant a convicted killer was automatically entitled to parole consideration after serving just two and a half decades. Not surprisingly, Joel, who had dispensed with the lives of others so easily, thought that was enough. Anything more, he believed, would deter any rehabilitative efforts. He also believed the death penalty was a waste of taxpayer money because convicted killers would be of better use to society as research subjects. Joel felt that invaluable data could be accumulated by examining their lives, and that could stop prospective killers from developing murderous impulses.

Soon after being elected in 1995, Governor George E. Pataki reinstated the death penalty, which had not been used in New York since 1963. There are presently five men on death row at the Clinton Correctional Facility, the same prison where Joel is currently housed in protective custody. One of the condemned men, a forty-seven-year-old former Long Island postal worker named Robert Shulman, was sentenced to death in 1998 for killing and dismembering three prostitutes. He was the first person to be tried under the serial killer section of the capital punishment law, stringent legislation that would certainly have landed Joel in the same place had it been in effect a few years earlier. While Joel claimed to have no interest in Shulman's case he did ask me to send any news clippings related to the case. He said he was interested in them only as possible ammunition for his own appeal.

Maher and the other prospective jurors were just settling in for a long day of waiting when official word came that they were being sent over to criminal court. She remembers hearing a collective gasp from the group, then felt her own heart begin to beat at a breakneck pace. "They started rounding everybody up and putting us on buses," she explained. "As nervous as everybody was, me included, I think down deep we wanted to be on that bus. Some of us just wanted to get a glance at the monster, others wanted to be picked so they could be the ones to say guilty."

The instant Maher entered the courtroom she was transfixed by the sight of the killer. Although his back was turned and he was looking down at the table as he furiously scribbled on a pad, he appeared as disheveled as in all of his newspaper photos. Despite having a highly developed narcissistic side, Joel was terrified of being on display in front of such a large audience. He much preferred to read about himself in newspapers or see himself on television than to socially interact with the public. By keeping his back turned and not looking up at the assembling jurors, he was in essence retreating back into the self-imposed isolation in which he had always felt so comfortable. But you can bet that had Joel been watching these formalities on television rather than having to sit through them in person, he would have been in his glory.

As apprehensive and nervous as she felt, Maher could not keep her eyes off Joel, and gawked at him as if he were a caged animal. She had expected him to have a commanding presence in person and was surprised to find otherwise. "I started to think if he turned around I would have been able to look him in the eye because he just seemed so harmless," she said. "If he was following me on the street, I would not have even been alarmed. You would think that by me knowing what he did my imagination would run wild, and I'd see him as a vicious monster. I was really surprised at what a little reaction I had. It is obvious that is why he got away with it for so long. So many of these killers are ordinary, so many of their neighbors are shocked when they get caught, so many of their friends say they never saw a sign. It was always hard for me to understand that, but I fully understand it now."

Finally a large group that included Maher was collectively asked the pivotal question about their ability to serve without prejudice and almost all, including Maher, were immediately removed from the panel. "They asked us if we could be unbiased in deciding the fate of an accused serial killer," recalled Maher. "As open-minded as I like to consider myself, I honestly answered that I could not. I wouldn't have been able to listen to anything about him unbiasedly, I would have just given him the death penalty [if it was an option at the time]. The fact that I would one day marry a police officer had no bearing on the matter. I didn't even know my future husband yet. I knew I could probably be unbiased with a guy accused of robbing a store or burglarizing a home, but what Rifkin did was too inexcusable. Everybody [potential jurors] I came with, except one man, was released. He was retained, but I don't know if he ever made it onto the actual jury."

Joel fired Michael Soshnick shortly after the pretrial hearings in December and Joel was now represented solely by John Lawrence, whose only previous experience was as a negligence lawyer. Joel's culpability was never in question. After all, he had clearly admitted to killing Tiffany Bresciani, as well as sixteen others. Even without his confessions, which had all been ruled admissible, the Bresciani case, the only murder for which he was currently on trial, seemed airtight. Convincing a skeptical jury that Joel was either legally insane or unable to appreciate the wrongfulness of his actions owing to mental disease or defect was going to be an arduous task, especially in traditionally conservative Nassau County.

To bolster his assertion that his client was insane, Lawrence hired Long Island–based psychiatrist Barbara R. Kirwin to examine Joel. She was better known for testifying on behalf of the prosecution, and she warned Lawrence that he was on a "kamikaze mission." "I'll do it for you, Jack," she told him. "But one shot in ten thousand this guy is the genuine article. He's probably a sexual psychopath, a Bundy or a Dahmer. There's little I could do for you other than suggest ways you might present the defense. Most likely what I'll find will be more supportive of the prosecution's case, and I'll probably wind up coming down on that side."

Much to her surprise, that was not how Kirwin came down. In an article entitled "The Truly Insane," Kirwin wrote later about visiting Joel over the course of several days in late 1993. She described him raising his "vacant, glazed eyes upward," an expression she would soon come to associate with him whenever she "asked him any question that required insight or abstraction." She said that she saw the "same inhuman look in the eyes of a milk shark" that she and several friends once rescued at a Long Island beach. It was a look that the press described as detached, bored, and uninterested, and would later be interpreted as proof of his evil, predatory nature and his lack of remorse. What made Joel even more of an enigma to Kirwin was the fact that he boasted he had "never thrown a punch in anger or defense," which she called a "curious contradiction for the confessed killer of seventeen prostitutes."

At one point in their discourse, Joel suddenly, inexplicably, and completely out of context, leaned toward Kirwin and almost whispered in her ear: "I have premonitions. I will die at sixty-nine. My father died at sixty-eight, outlived his mother by one year." After a pause, he continued, "I predicted my arrest. I was thirty-four, which is half of sixty-eight. I knew that number seventeen would be the last because two times seventeen equals thirty-four. I even calculated the extra days for leap years, like for the year the Dolphins played the Super Bowl."

After giving Joel the Minnesota Multiphasic Personality Inventory (MMPI), a test designed to determine psychopathology, Kirwin asked a colleague who was unaware that Joel was the subject to score the test. He described the subject as a "near classic psychotic" and asked, "Who is this guy? I never saw elevations like this. They're off the scale." When Kirwin herself plotted Joel's MMPI scores on the profile sheet, she called them "the most pathological test results that I had ever encountered in nearly twenty years of administering this test in parole offices, prisons, and the back wards of mental hospitals."

I once took the MMPI during a background investigation for a sensitive job and I remember thinking how easy it would have been to manipulate had I been so inclined. Certainly, if the subject answered truthfully, it would detect insanity or psychopathology in a second. Because the test was loaded with questions about hearing voices and wanting to kill someone, I believe that any relatively sane person could choose to come out looking like either a docile lamb or a snarling psychopath. There is always the possibility that Joel was completely truthful, but that would contradict much of the information he gave other inquisitors over the years.

Joe Piraino believes the only reason I found the MMPI so laughable was because I was clearly not suffering from any mental defects and was in fact sane. "It is a very comprehensive evaluation," he said. "It has no shortage of validity indicators to determine if someone is being truthful or not. One might think they are outsmarting it, but they will be tripped up as the test progresses. The test is a very good indicator of cognition, depression, narcissism, volatile behavior, high risk behavior, and how people perceive themselves or are perceived by others."

The prosecution countered with a well-known forensic psychiatrist named Dr. Park Elliot Dietz of Newport Beach, California, who spent four days interviewing Joel at the Nassau County jail. A nationally recognized authority on serial killers, Dietz also testified for the prosecution at the trials of Jeffrey Dahmer and Arthur Shawcross, and he gained international acclaim by testifying in the John Hinckley case after Hinckley tried to assassinate President Ronald Reagan in 1981. Dietz's analysis could not have differed more from Kirwin's.

While he saw Joel as a sexual sadist and necrophiliac who also suffered from mood swings and personality disorders, he was certain that Joel was sane and had known exactly what he was doing during each and every homicide. He also insisted that there was no evidence of a thinking disorder; in fact Joel, whose IQ was about 130, was able to perform such tasks as naming United States presidents in reverse order all the way back to William Howard Taft, who served from 1909–13.

Had Joel's own statements been ruled inadmissible, the conflicting opinions of the doctors might have given him a better shot at convincing a jury he was crazy. But the composed manner in which he described his horrific actions would be difficult to overcome. Joel, who had done plenty of research in the law library, had even changed his appearance in an attempt to positively influence the jury. But it would take more than simply trimming his shaggy hair and putting on a suit to convince the seven-man, five-woman jury that he was just a troubled boy next door who happened to be insane.

16

"THE DEFENDANT ACTED WITH UNPARAL-
leled evil and depravity," said ADA Fred Klein in his
opening statement, as Joel, wearing his father's
shoes and college ring for spiritual support, seemed
preoccupied with an imaginary spot on the wall. "He
is a sadistic serial killer who achieved sexual satisfaction by strangling women. He got a sexual charge
out of thinking about strangling young women from
a young age. The defendant is a very bright guy, with
very high intelligence. He was well aware of the consequences of his actions. Sure, maybe Joel Rifkin
had an unhappy childhood, kids ridiculed him, and
he didn't get along with women, but he knows what
he did was wrong. He got caught red-handed, and
now he's using and abusing the concept of mental
illness."

"I will not make light of what happened," countered Lawrence. "The taking of Miss Bresciani's life was a senseless, horrifying act, as it was for his other victims. Mr. Rifkin is a paranoid schizophrenic and has suffered from the disease since early childhood. His illness became uncontrollable after his father's death in 1987. The monster inside of him took control and caused him to act out in very macabre ways. Joel has lived in the twilight zone, unable to relate to reality, overcome by a compulsion of violent images toward women, a compulsion that took control of his life."

Joel seemed distanced and uninterested as the state's first witness, Tiffany's mother, Cheryl Bresciani, took the stand and told the court about the last time she had seen her daughter alive—back home in Louisiana nine months before her death. Totally unaffected by her testimony, Joel seemed equally unruffled by the presence of family members of at least three other of his victims in the spectator seats. His mind seemed to drift throughout the testimony of the state's second witness, Laura Borruso, who danced with Tiffany at the Big Top Lounge and said she had seen Joel there on several occasions. This is yet another curious contradiction of Joel's own words. Hadn't he told me, as well as a national television audience on the *Leeza* show, that once he started attaching names to his victims and seeing their family members at court proceedings he began to realize the enormity of his actions?

By the time state trooper Sean Ruane, who along with Trooper Spaargaren initiated the car chase that led to Joel's arrest, appeared on the stand after lunch as the state's third witness, Joel, his chin cupped in his hand, was fast asleep. A reporter later questioned Lawrence about his client's apathy toward both his victims and the prospect of long-term incarceration. Lawrence came up with an explanation that proves when it comes to legal arguments, anything can be disputed sensibly as long as the orator can keep a straight face.

"We have lodged a formal complaint with the judge," he explained, his face solemn and serious. "Joel Rifkin is allergic to the nitrates in the bologna sandwich that was waiting for him at lunchtime today. While I advised him not to eat it and to only eat the bread, he was hungry."

As unprecedented as the baloney nitrate excuse was, an even more bizarre defense was being orchestrated in a courtroom down the hall. The late radical lawyer, William Kunstler, planned to use a "black rage" defense for Colin Ferguson, who was once again stealing Joel's thunder. The basis for the defense, which had already been argued in Los Angeles in the aftermath of the Rodney King riots, suggested that Ferguson was a persecuted immigrant and that he was sent into a rage because of the oppressive way he was treated by White America. Reporters flocked to that courtroom, leaving Joel to snooze in relative privacy and Klein to tenaciously try the beginning of a sensational murder case in relative anonymity. Interest in the Rifkin case eventually revived on the day his only defense witness, Dr. Kirwin, was scheduled to take the stand. She was Joel's last hope, the only person at this point who could conceivably keep him from going to jail for the rest of his life. But her appearance was postponed for several days because of a national day of mourning proclaimed by President Bill Clinton for the death of former President Richard Nixon. Even after reinventing himself as a modern-day Jack the Ripper and being the defendant in what he perceived as Long Island's trial of the century, Joel was once again playing second fiddle.

When the trial resumed it became a heated battle between Kirwin and Dietz, the imported hired gun who countered everything Kirwin said. Kirwin explained that Joel was a paranoid schizophrenic, as well as delusional, grandiose, hallucinatory, and incoherent. "His mind is like a videotape in that it fast forwards and then suddenly rewinds," she explained. "There is no normal time sequence in his thinking."

Dietz agreed that Joel suffered from mood disorder but asserted that he was a sexual sadist and a necrophiliac as well. He didn't believe that Joel had a thinking disorder that would have prevented him from knowing right from wrong when he killed Tiffany Bresciani. The fact that he went to such great lengths to cover up his crimes was proof of that. While Joel's actions might have seemed insane to a normal person, they were not the work of a crazy man. The fact that he was so sloppy and disorganized, added Dietz, was a protective mechanism that began in early childhood when his mother said he would have to clean his room before he could go out to play. Rather than go outside and face his tormentors, Joel chose to live among his own disorder where he could, in essence, wrap himself up in an imaginary cocoon.

Kirwin said Joel's statements about having sex with dead bodies were delusional; Dietz said they were not because Joel had told him he stroked and fondled the dead bodies of Barbara Jacobs, Lorraine Orvieto, and Mary Catherine Williams. Kirwin said Joel regularly had hallucinations, a symptom of schizophrenia; Dietz said Joel often heard "whispers" that sometimes spoke to him, but because he knew the voice was coming from within, it was not hallucinatory. Furthermore, said Dietz, hearing whispers and having internal conversations is far from unusual for someone as socially isolated as Joel. Kirwin said Joel gave "grossly inappropriate responses to interviewers' questions"; Dietz said he did not. Kirwin said Joel had no sexual perversions; Dietz insisted Joel was a sexual sadist who loved to inflict pain on women and then engage in sexual activity with their corpses.

Kirwin said Joel had trouble perceiving time; Dietz said he was able to give a coherent linear progression of his life. Kirwin suggested that Joel told different doctors different things; Dietz countered by listing many of the consistencies in his various accounts. Kirwin based her determination of Joel's schizophrenia on the results of the MMPI test; Dietz said it was clear that Joel was trying to manipulate the results. Kirwin said Joel kept jewelry and other belongings of his victims as a frame of reference because of his problems with time; Dietz said he kept them to use as nostalgic mementos and masturbatory material.

Kirwin said a letter Joel wrote to his attorneys imploring them to arrange a movie deal and publishing rights for his story was delusional; Dietz said that it showed he was in touch with reality and was clear evidence of his rampant narcissism. Kirwin said Joel's thinking disorder prevented him from knowing that what he was doing was wrong when he killed Bresciani, while Dietz said the exact opposite was true. He pointed to the fact that Joel went to great lengths to hide the bodies, was adept at lying, led police on a high-speed chase, and perhaps most glaringly, moved his car away from a potential witness—the man doing his early morning Tai Chi exercises—while in the midst of killing Tiffany Bresciani.

While a schizophrenic regularly experiences hallucinations, delusions, and illogical thinking, a schizotypal personality, which Dietz believed more appropriately fit Joel, is usually considered odd, has few friends, and is thought of as a quintessential loner. Such people also often have strange perceptions; in Joel's case these were manifested by his extreme belief in superstition. After all, did he not believe that some strong, unseen energy made the head of Susie, victim number one, roll onto the golf course? Was it not the same negative energy that made him forget to attach a license plate to his truck, thus leading to his arrest? What about the strange energy that made him perform the following ritual after so many of his murders?

"I almost always drove the body past where I picked it up," he told me during a prison visit. "I explained this as letting the spirit go where it was in its territory kind of thing." Told that this could be interpreted as a bizarre act of kindness, Joel was not sure if he saw it that way. "Could be," he mused. "It goes on the heading of odd thinking. You are not necessarily rational during these things. So what makes no sense to me now, made sense to me then."

"The fact that Rifkin went to such great lengths to avoid capture is indicative of him being sane, at least from a legal standpoint," said Joe Piraino. "Even though he had fantasized about killing for years, he only became a killer once he started murdering people. There was never any doubt in his mind that what he was doing was wrong. He was not like a man raised in an organized crime culture, who commits what we call career killings because he views them as a means to an end in his chosen profession. There is a big difference here that is lost on some people.

"Mob wannabes fantasize about killing people," he continued. "There are some people who are turned on by fantasies of sex with children or are aroused by the fantasy of killing people indiscriminately. But only after those thoughts become actions have they crossed the line. We cannot penalize people for bad thoughts. We can only penalize them for bad actions. Rifkin killed because of a lack of his own impulse control, much the way a pedophile cannot refrain from having sex with children. Serial killers, pedophiles, and career killers might all be equally cold, calculating, and remorseless, but in most cases they are unquestionably sane. The only difference with the career killers is the fact that they are not usually ruled by their impulses, while the others almost always are. As strange as it seems, the only way Rifkin could have control in his life was by killing. In this one area, he would always know the outcome. By having supreme control over the lives of his victims, he began to see himself as God-like."

In closing arguments, Fred Klein painted Joel as a cold, calculating, remorseless killer, who preyed upon his victims for no other reason than to satisfy his sadistic and insatiable sexual desires. Lawrence once again painted him as a schizophrenic, making him, from a criminal perspective at least, not responsible for his actions. "Mr. Rifkin has many problems," Dietz told the jury. "He is sick, but not insane. He knew exactly what he was doing and he did it."

The three-week trial officially ended on May 9, 1994, when, after just two and a half hours of deliberations, the jury forewoman announced that Joel was guilty of murder, as well as a felony count of reckless endangerment for leading police on the high-speed chase.

Later that day, Jeanne Rifkin, who had been silent up to that time, spoke with reporters at her home. Speaking with the same dignity that would become her trademark, the emotionally devastated woman said her "heart went out" to the families of her son's victims. And that she had already resigned herself to the likelihood that he would never be free to hurt again. "Nobody would want that, neither would I," she said. "But he will always be my son. All those years don't go away with the snap of a finger."

17

WHILE JOEL WAS STILL HOUSED IN NAS-
sau County, he was regularly attending court hearings throughout the metropolitan area for many of
the other murders he had confessed to. One police officer who drew transport duty from an outside jurisdiction was amazed at how downright
ordinary Joel seemed and how disarmingly pleasant he was. At one point they were making small
talk and the officer, who knew of Joel's interest in
horticulture, began asking him about planting
bushes in the hard clay ground at his newly purchased vacation home in the Pocono Mountains in
eastern Pennsylvania.

"The guy just opened up and seemed to take
great pleasure in helping me out," said the officer.
"I really did not expect an answer, I was just trying

to keep things loose. He was being represented by a lawyer for the homicide in my jurisdiction, so I was unable to question him. I was just babysitting him throughout the day and wanted to put us both at ease. But he started talking about the difference between perennials and annuals and how to overcome my problem. It was like I was talking to Good Neighbor Joel."

To this day the officer, a nineteen-year law enforcement veteran, has to keep reminding himself that he was in the company of the most prolific killer in New York State history. "I'm not naive by any stretch, but Joel seemed more like a friendly neighbor than anything else," he said. "It was like he called me for help after getting picked up at a DWI [driving while intoxicated] checkpoint while driving home from his Christmas office party. This guy seemed to be as gentle as a puppy dog."

As normal as Joel seemed, the transport officer did see a stranger side of him as the day wore on. During the many hours Joel spent in the holding pen, he did not seem to have a care in the world. While many prisoners pace, sleep, or try to make small talk with their jailers, Joel's only preoccupation was with a tiny gash in the wall. For hours on end he fixated on it, mindlessly picking at it with his thumbnail. By the time he was done, about three hours later, it was about as wide as a quarter and twice as deep.

"He was very friendly and would enthusiastically respond to questions," said the officer. "But when we weren't talking to him, he would just zero in on that crack. It seemed like he was hypnotized by it. At first I didn't realize what progress he was making, but when I saw that it went from a barely visible slash to a significantly sized opening I was very surprised. Other than the fact that he seemed like a people pleaser, he was completely at ease and at peace with himself. I have never dealt with a more polite or well-mannered prisoner. He was very engaging, even likable."

A detective from the same department who transported Joel on a separate occasion had a similar assessment. "He seemed no different than you and me," he said. "It was like he wanted the same things out of life as us, appreciated the same things as us, and was as surprised as us that he was in all this trouble. At one point he even pointed out a weak link on the daisy [handcuff] chain. I looked at it closely and, sure enough, it was weakening. In police work you learn to expect the unexpected, but this guy really took me by surprise. I've been around long enough to not be easily surprised, but he sure surprised me."

A female court officer in yet another jurisdiction agreed. She was handling the arraignment for one of Joel's murders and expected to be at least somewhat emotionally affected by his presence.

"We handle dozens of defendants every day, and they all become faceless after a while," she recalled. "But this was someone who had been on the front pages of the newspapers for weeks. We had extra officers in the room in case he tried to make a break for it or some family members of his victims tried to extract their own revenge. Our adrenaline was pumping as we waited for this shackled beast to be brought before the judge for his arraignment. Instead we saw this sloppy, unkempt, totally goofy-looking guy who most women probably could have knocked over with a cold stare."

Although Joel was being passed around to various jurisdictions like a prize bull, Suffolk County would have the first go at him after his conviction in the Bresciani homicide. He was transferred to that jail on the day after his Nassau conviction and began another arduous regimen of pretrial hearings for the murders of Leah Evans and Lauren Marquez. His new attorney, Martin Efman, relied on a concept called adopted child syndrome to bolster the defense's contention that Joel might have been born with genetic neurological damage. Although the sealed adoption records might have shed some light on Joel's aberrational behavior, Jeanne Rifkin fought hard to prevent them from being opened. The way she saw it, there had already been enough tears and bloodshed brought on by her son's actions. If, in fact, his birth parents were still alive, it would just mean that two more innocent people would be dragged into what already seemed like an unending tragedy.

At the Suffolk suppression hearings Joel took the stand and insisted that he had asked for an attorney no less than twenty times during his interrogation, thereby negating any incriminating statements he made about his involvement in all the murders except Bresciani's. Under the Miranda rule, police are required to cease questioning once a suspect asks for a lawyer. In my many years of police work, countless defendants, for crimes ranging from minimal offenses to murder, have agreed to talk without the presence of an attorney. Most of them even offered to chronicle their version of events in written form. Inevitably, nearly every one of them will eventually insist that they were coerced into making these written or oral statements.

It would become such an issue that I would go to great lengths to ward off their accusations before they were even able to make them. Once, an attorney for two brothers facing murder charges in a Brooklyn street killing implied that I had withheld food from his clients until they gave me the confessions I wanted. Knowing what a strong case I had against the brothers, which was only enhanced by their written statements, I was prepared for an all-out assault by the defense. As a result I went so far as to file a follow-up report stating the options I gave the brothers for lunch—pizza or burgers—what flavor of soda they ordered, and how many slices of pizza were left uneaten. I even documented that I had asked them if they wanted to save the remaining slices to be eaten later and that they declined. The lawyer, who foolishly had not read that report prior to questioning me, seemed embarrassed when it was brought to his attention. The questioning ceased immediately, and the brothers pled guilty shortly afterward.

Knowing Joel's propensity for talking, I am inclined to believe he confessed of his own volition. Even if his statements were ruled inadmissible in Suffolk and negatively affected future proceedings in other jurisdictions, they still would have had no impact on the Bresciani guilty verdict. At one point in the hearings state police investigator Thomas Capers testified that he asked Joel if he had killed other people and the defendant had remained silent. Responding to the investigator's gentle prodding, Joel finally blurted out, "One or a hundred, what's the difference?"

The difference was that the Suffolk judge denied Joel's bid to suppress the confessions and the second of many more trials began soon. After undergoing another battery of court-appointed psychological tests, Joel, never much of a fighter to begin with, elected to take the path of least resistance. He pled guilty to the top charges in both murders and received two consecutive sentences of twenty-five years to life, meaning he would have to serve at least fifty years on those cases alone before being eligible for parole. Coupled with the minimum sentence of thirty-three and a half years that he got for his conviction in the Bresciani case, Joel was already looking at more than eight decades in prison. And he still had thirteen other murders that had not yet been adjudicated. "It is important that this man will never be able to harm anyone again," said Evans's mother, Sue.

Joel appeared unaffected by the lengthy sentences and, as self-centered as always, seemed more concerned with the surgery he had undergone to remove a cyst on his thigh at Central Suffolk Hospital in Riverhead just weeks earlier. "My being here today with an open three-and-a-half-inch surgical incision is a flagrant violation of the court's oath and responsibility," he complained at his sentencing. "This defendant sees no reason in law or logic that compels this defendant to be here on this date when the court could have easily postponed this matter for the two weeks for the wound to heal properly."

The judge, John J. J. Jones, was unmoved. "Your condition warranted release from the hospital," he intoned. "The court sees no reason to delay the sentence."

Prosecutor Michael Ahearn, who was also the chief of the Suffolk County DA's office, was even less sympathetic. "People have those cut out in a doctor's office," he scoffed. "He views himself as the victim, as the person who has been put upon in this case. He used those women, he abused those women, and he ultimately took their lives."

In late November Joel pled guilty to the murder of Iris Sanchez in Queens, then, just days later, entered guilty pleas in Brooklyn and received maximum consecutive sentences for the killings of Lorraine Orvieto, Mary Ann Holloman, and the still unidentified third woman, all of whom had been found stuffed into steel drums over a three-month period in 1992. When he appeared for sentencing in the Queens case on January 25, 1996, Carol DeLeon, the sister of Iris Sanchez, was in attendance with her husband, her three-year-old daughter, and her mother. Making an impassioned plea for justice, she told the court, "He has shown no remorse for what he has done. For you Rifkin, you will rot in hell forever, and the rest of your life."

Judge Robert Hanophy agreed and quickly added another twenty-five years to the more than 175 years Joel was already serving. "It is not in my power to give Mr. Rifkin the sentence he deserves," said the judge. "In case there is such a thing as reincarnation, I want you to spend your second life in prison."

Joel, who was sporting a black eye from a beating he received a few days earlier in the day room at the New York City jail compound at Rikers Island, was a lot more vocal than he had been at any of his other hearings. He even tried to offer up an explanation for his actions. "Everyone had a theory but no one knows the real me, and I have given up hoping that anyone ever will," he said in a barely audible voice. "You may all think I am nothing but a monster, and you are right. Part of me must be." He then added that there were other serial killers just like him "walking the streets right now."

JOEL WAS ASSIGNED INMATE NUMBER 95-A6514, the numerical designation he will carry with him for the rest of his natural life, when he arrived at the Attica Correctional Facility in February 1996. Located in the remote flatlands of western New York State, about sixty miles east of Buffalo, Attica is a Dickensian fortress-like structure that is universally known for housing the worst of the worst, as well as being the last stop for many of the state's most notorious prisoners. David Berkowitz, who was better known as Son of Sam, was housed there until a fellow inmate slashed him from ear to ear, and Mark David Chapman, the killer of John Lennon, has spent his entire twenty-one years of incarceration there.

Attica's fearsome reputation resulted from an

infamous 1971 siege and takeover by inmates that left twenty-nine prisoners and eleven hostages dead. Much has been written about that horrific incident, which one investigatory commission described as "the bloodiest encounter between Americans since the Civil War." During the six-minute period when most of the inmates and prison employees were killed, officers had fired more than two thousand rounds of ammunition. The incident left an enduring mark on the collective psyche of the American public. Three decades later the word Attica is still synonymous with the precarious line between violence and justice.

While he was never housed with the general population, Joel did initially have limited contact with other prisoners. But his presence soon proved to be extremely disruptive. Other inmates, who decided to settle society's score by making his life unbearable, regularly taunted and threatened him. "You're locked in, but there was a lot of feces throwing and stuff like that," Joel explained. "You get right down to the primate level here. A lot of chest beating, rattling the cage, and urine throwing. It's like the ape house. Classy guys."

But the taunting actually served him well because it enabled him to find comfort, as he always did, in his own little world. Life was actually much easier for him without the burden of trying to fit in. On many levels Joel had not progressed much from his days as a schoolyard victim. He was still able to keep the world at bay by retreating into his own secret place. He had never been included before and he had no motivation to be included now.

Joel was soon placed in an isolated cell in involuntary protective custody (IPC), a virtual prison within the prison. He was living under the same conditions as inmates who were being disciplined for such rule violations as fighting, assault on staff, and gang involvement. The inmates were locked in their cells for twenty-three hours a day. Unlike the regular prison population, which is allowed time at the steel rack in the prison yard or in front of a television set, IPC prisoners are allowed very little. The only packages they can receive are new or used magazines and books, only ten of which can be in their cell at any given time.

They have no phone privileges, only one in-cell sick call, a limited commissary, and little or no psychiatric counseling. They are allowed out of their cells for one hour of recreation a day in a yard that Joel describes as "a square room, seventeen heel-to-toe paces on the diagonal, which is probably smaller than a regulation [boxing] ring apron. The only view is straight up to the sky." Never a physical fitness enthusiast, Joel rarely left his cell except for three ten-minute cold-water showers per week. Most of his time at Attica was spent reading—about twelve books a month—or drawing, which had become a passion.

While Joel found the isolation of IPC comforting initially, it soon became difficult for him to handle. Although the inmates were never in physical contact with each other, they were able to assert their aggression in other ways. Because the steel beds were welded into the walls, an angry inmate could literally rattle the cages of his neighbors by pounding the walls with his fists. When that occurred, which was often, Joel would move his mattress to the floor.

"There [was] a lot of noise [in the section]," said Joel. "You just bark and someone will bark back at you and the whole place will listen and some guys will jump in. Generally it's about nothing. They'll talk about sports, they'll kindergarten insult each other."

The long hours alone left Joel with plenty of time for introspection, which was never one of his strong points. He lamented to me that he became more adept at it than he would have liked. "Occasionally [I'd] take a book up just to turn that off," he said. Not surprisingly, his thoughts were in no way occupied with all the madness he had perpetrated, only in attempting to learn what had driven him to it. He was particularly intrigued with recent scientific studies that suggested there is such a thing as a criminal brain, and that some people are actually "wired" to commit violent antisocial acts like rape and murder.

This controversial study by Adrian Raine, a professor of psychology at the University of Southern California, was published in the *Archives of General Psychiatry.* Because it linked violent, antisocial behavior to a specific anatomical abnormality in the brain, it has pitted theorists who attribute criminal behavior to sociological factors such as child abuse and poverty against those now linking criminality with biological origins. Raine found that a large number of violent criminals had a reduced amount of gray matter in the prefrontal lobe of the brain, the area just behind the eyes that is known to be involved in judgment and impulse control. He contends that "individuals who are antisocial, impulsive, reckless, lacking in remorse, and who commit crimes and violence have, on average, eleven percent less gray matter in the prefrontal cortex than normal subjects.

"We are beginning to uncover some of the brain basis for violence," said Raine. "We've done a lot of research in the past on social factors. But we've systematically ignored the biological part of the equation."

Raine said his study was never meant to establish a cause-and-effect relationship between the brain defect and a tendency toward violence, but his research is consistent with previous studies suggesting that damage and chemical imbalances within the brain may play a role in some violent behavior. What he is certain of is the fact that reduced gray matter "increases the probability that the individual will become violent," if combined with such social factors as child abuse, improper parenting, and poverty that create the "toxic mix" typical of most violent offenders. "We are only now beginning to identify the biological pieces of the jigsaw puzzle," he said.

When asked directly if there is such a thing as a criminal brain, an idea worthy of a grade-B horror movie, Raine was unequivocal in his response. "If by a criminal brain you mean brain factors that predispose and increase the odds of someone becoming criminal, then yes," he reasoned. "If you mean that every criminal has a biological brain deficit the answer is no."

"I can agree with the theory that certain people might be born with brain abnormalities that might make them more prone to violence than someone else," said Ray Pierce. "But there have to be other factors involved as well. If such a person has a good role model or mentor and is guided in such a way, in many cases the taste for violence could be eradicated. I don't buy into the premise that some sane people are just born bad. If you study almost every killer out there, there are factors that led them to the path they chose. In Joel's case, you just can't dismiss the fact that he was picked on almost every day of his life. He wasn't born being picked on. That all happened later."

Joe Piraino believes that frontal lobe damage, coupled with other environmental factors, can easily retard a person's psychological and physical development. In his opinion, the fact that Joel did not exhibit any traditional early antisocial behavior—namely juvenile delinquency—indicates that, while he might have had a predisposition to violence, it took time for him to act on his impulses. "Once Rifkin's inhibitors were weakened, the monster in him was finally let loose," he said. "That is not to say it was not always there. The fact that he lived a secretive fantasy life for so long is very telling. While it took a series of events to make him hatch, the propensity for such violence was always present. Once he broke out of his eggshell with the first killing, the monster was born. Most serial killers are not bug-eyed, scary-looking people. They get away with their crimes by hiding in a cloak of normalcy. While we only remember them for their misdeeds, the bizarre behaviors upon which their crimes are predicated constitute only a small fraction of their total behavior."

Perhaps the best known example linking brain lesions and abnormalities to multiple murder is the case of Charles Whitman, the sniper who killed sixteen people and wounded thirty more in 1966 at the University of Texas in Austin. After he was shot and killed by police, an autopsy revealed a malignant tumor in the area of the brain associated with rage. In a more recent example, renowned attorney Johnnie Cochran managed to keep former heavyweight boxing champion Riddick Bowe from serving a federal prison sentence for interstate domestic violence by successfully arguing in a North Carolina court that his actions were caused, in great part, by frontal lobe damage incurred in the ring. Bowe was found guilty of abducting his estranged wife and five children and then driving them to Virginia in an ill-fated attempt at reconciliation. During the terror ride, Bowe opened a bag filled with duct tape, a buck knife, and pepper spray and announced, "I came prepared." In Bowe's last fight, against Andrew Golota in December 1996, he was hit with over four hundred punches. While he was somewhat articulate prior to the fight, during the postfight interview his speech was nearly incomprehensible. Since then, it has gotten progressively worse.

Joel, who has always maintained that what propelled him to kill is as much of a mystery to him as everyone else, said he would find it refreshing to learn there might be some sort of neurological or scientific explanation for his actions. "All throughout the trials I was accused of malingering and fakery and faking insanity," he said. "To me a Pet Scan [a neurological exam to determine prefrontal lobe damage] is like an X ray. If the bone is broken, it's broken. You can't fake a broken bone. If there's something not working upstairs, I didn't fake it. If that can help the next generation of kids, if we can spot these problems and treat them chemically, [it would be] cutting edge, pioneer."

He addressed the possibility of keeping prospective killers from embarking on murderous paths long before they even realize what they are capable of. "I heard this amazing thing this morning [where] this guy with mice is growing new brain cells and making a smarter mouse," he explained. "It's gonna be in a magazine. So we're getting to this stage where we can manipulate what we're born with. So if there's an area that's not functioning, maybe we can get it to function. There was also another study where they did something to tadpoles, where they found that the neurons keep re-entangling themselves and shifting all throughout your life. So maybe this area affects conscience and planning and can be woken up, get some neurons in there."

Joel is fully cognizant of his inability to feel genuine remorse for his victims and their families and is eager to find out why. "[If a doctor] wants to come over here and take me up to Strong Memorial [Hospital in nearby Rochester, New York] and do a Pet [Scan], fine," he said. "If another doctor wants to try this chemical injection and try his theory, I'm a guinea pig. I mean, I'm here. I'm available."

Asked if offering his brain for forensic, psychiatric, or medical research would bring him any amount of redemption, he seemed somewhat uninterested before referring to the recent upsurge in executions by individual states. "Yeah, yeah, if it works out that way," he said. "But they have a very large [guinea pig] population [on Death Row] and unfortunately their population tends to die off at a very accelerated rate now. They really can't do a study in Texas because they don't have the available material."

Another way Joel passed the time was to write to legislators and newspapers about the dangers of the streets, and how his wealth of knowledge could possibly save the lives of countless potential victims who might inadvertently fall into the clutches of someone like him. If his words hadn't been so clearly motivated by narcissism, they might have indicated that he had developed a bit of a social conscience. Except that the beneficiaries of his actions were all potential murder victims who were not fortunate enough to have any political muscle behind them, the very type of victim he had preyed upon so expertly.

"During my time on the street, thirteen female

prostitutes disappeared from the Eleventh to Twelfth [Street], Second to First Avenue square block [area], and no one noticed," he wrote to me in a letter dated January 26, 1999. "Not one word in the press. But when two male transgender prostitutes are killed there is press (probably a lot more than I am aware of from in here). The difference is one group has a political action group and the other doesn't. The life of both is equal, but if a predator is stalking the Lower West Side all of the press and neighborhood activity makes it very difficult for him to function."

He enclosed a copy of a letter he had sent to numerous upstate New York newspapers in response to the 1999 Columbine High School massacre in Colorado. One was printed in the *Batavia News* under the headline "Violence too profitable."

Editor:

I live with the sons of America, the lost and forgotten sons. My neighbor at 16 shot another teen four times. I hear talk everyday of respecting the "Gun Game," and "Double Clip" used in greetings. My perspective is now one where I witness daily the influence that commercial-like mass media violence has had on my fellow residents of Attica Prison. They brag loud and proud not only of how young they were when they lost their sexual virginity but also their gun virginity. They speak of the different guns that they have held with the same affection that other men have for past girlfriends.

As one whose crimes were in part influenced by violent film images, and one who like you has become a vicarious witness to the tragically repeated school slayings, I now attempt to remind you as parents of your responsibility to limit your child's exposure to repetitive violence. The entertainment, computer game and toy makers earn far too much profit from the sale of violence to ever curtail it on their own. But by boycotting, refusing to buy the product, we can affect the content of the product. The recent mass strategy of anti-tobacco and teen smoking needs to be focused on our children before another school becomes a free-fire killing zone.

Joel Rifkin
Attica Correctional Facility

Although I had been vehemently warned by both Joe Piraino and Ray Pierce that Joel's new-found sense of charity had more to do with his ungratified ego than anything else, initially I wasn't so sure. Because he had been truthful on so many occasions when it was of no help to him whatsoever, like when he told Geraldo Rivera that he was

unable to feel remorse, I had to give him the benefit of the doubt.

I still had difficulty with the concept of people
being born evil. If medical tests bore out that Joel
did indeed have prefrontal brain damage, wouldn't
that at least offer some explanation for his actions?
While it would make him no less culpable, it
might offer him some comfort and provide me
with some semblance of understanding. As a
guardian of the public, I think I was angry with
myself for not being able to see it coming, even all
those years before.

"I always admitted my guilt from day one," Joel
told me. "The Nassau trial was a housing trial—
asylum or prison. Did I know my actions were
wrong at the time I did them? I don't think so.
Was I aware of my actions at the time I did them?
Yes. Now I don't have an obvious injury. I don't
have a lesion. I don't have scarring from being hit.
I think that the frontal lobe problem just makes
you odd, and that begins the whole cycle. The odd
guy gets picked on. I once said this to my mom,
that when you watch the nature shows a lion will
run into a herd of zebra and before he even gets
there he knows which one he's going after. And
[it's] usually the infirm, the young, or the weak.
And I think the bully has that same sense. He can
walk into a playground and he can sense who the
easy targets are. And they say that with street

crimes, like muggers can pick out the little old lady who's not gonna resist, and know the one that's gonna whack him over the head with the purse. You know, it's a sense. I think I just had victim written on me when I was in school."

Asked if he used that same selection process when picking his own victims, he was a bit more circumspect, while continuing to refer to his killings as if they were a game of skill. "I don't know if it was that or if it was just . . . some of them did fight back," he responded. "Two of them are still walking around. I don't know if I was good at selection."

Nor does he think his actions in the immediate aftermath of the killings were in any way indicative of a man operating in a fully functional state. "By legal definition, at the time of the crime, yeah [I think I was insane]," he explained. "Disposing of the body hours later or days later is not the same as in the movies when a hit man does a hit, the gloves come off, the rifle gets dropped right there, and he walks away. He doesn't run away because he knows he'll get arrested if he doesn't completely disassociate from the evidence. I took the evidence with me. I mean it's a totally different thing."

Once again Joel seemed to be trying to craft a script that would enable him to disavow responsibility. I believed this was because of his narcissism and my feelings intensified when he sent me a handwritten announcement of a Discovery Channel broadcast called *The Mind of a Killer* in the fall of 1999. On the show Joel was put through a battery of on-camera tests to determine the extent of his frontal lobe damage. Joel truly believed he was about to become a star.

. . . BLEEP! . . . BLEEP! . . . BLEEP! . . .

The Mind of a Killer Discovery Channel Saturday

November 27th!

(That be me)

19

JOEL DID NOT GET THE ANSWERS HE
would have liked from his televised examination.
The tests were inconclusive and he was even accused by one of the doctors of being deceptive in
some of his responses. With that avenue for redemption seemingly closed, Joel turned his atten-
tions to a concept that had come to him like an
epiphany a few years earlier in the Suffolk County
jail. He would now try to pass himself off as a
sheep in wolf's clothing, a white knight who would
go to great lengths to provide a safe haven for prostitutes in order to save them from monsters like
himself.

He got the idea when he overheard correction
officers discussing a *Penthouse* magazine story that
described a chess game between him and a fellow

inmate named John Esposito. Esposito was awaiting trial for the unlawful imprisonment of a young
girl named Katie Beers, whom he had hidden in a
secret dungeon he had constructed under his
house. Although Joel had reveled in his notoriety
in the past, he says it finally hit him for the first
time just how big a celebrity inmate he was.

"I realized then that whatever it is I do is going
to get attention," he explained. Determined to
show the world "that something good can come
out of a tragedy," he began feverishly filling out
index cards with ideas that would later become
the proposal for the Oholah House Foundation, a
non-profit organization that would fund an after-
detox home and educational facility for former addict prostitutes. Looking for a name that would
have some degree of allegorical significance, he
chose *oholah*, which Joel said was a Hebrew word
for sanctuary. It is also the name of a biblical prostitute in chapter twenty-three of the Book of
Ezekiel who was murdered because of her amoral
behavior. "A sanctuary is a place of refuge, asylum
or protection," Joel stated on the cover of his
handwritten twenty-one-page manifesto. "A house
is a place of shelter; a home a place were [sic] people are cared for; thus Oholah House."

Joel drew on information from social workers,
attorneys, a television program about a Canadian
shelter for anorexic girls, and the scores of prosti-

tutes he had come in contact with for more than fifteen years, and the project quickly expanded to take on a life of its own in Joel's mind. The television documentary struck a particularly sensitive chord with Joel, because the low self-esteem that afflicted the girls was all too familiar to him. Problems with his self-image had dogged him since his family made the traumatic and fateful move to Long Island from their Rockland County home three decades earlier.

The following quotes were taken as is from Joel's handwritten Oholah proposal.

"A lot of the feelings you get with the girls is total worthlessness," said Joel. "Detox alone does not work without a new attitude and new capabilities. Oholah House would provide job skills training, GED, home economics, and other practical daily survival skills needed for a recovered street addict to maintain a more normal type of life style. Oholah House is not for every streetwalker but for those who truely want a change of life. As things existed prior to my arresst there was no true way out of the street life. I believe that a project like Oholah House could provide that way out."

Voluntary residence in the house would last from eighteen to twenty-four months, and only women dedicated to changing their lives would be eligible. "To achieve this singular goal a person needs to become self-sufficient so that they are capable of caring for themselves and family," the outline stated. "To achieve that end a program needs to be developed around a dedicated staff of both volunteers and professionals. A program should be created of 18 months to 24 months in duration that would intergrate the following: Counciling, Housing, 12 step, Job skills & placement (in or out of house), Legal Advise, Health & Mental (care and council), Home Skills, Parenting skills, Money Management, GED or 2 year College (or both), Social Skills, Family counsiling, Alonon, Family reunions, Buddy or Sisterhoods, Homecomings or reunions."

While Joel believed "the resident population should be kept small (twenty would be an ideal number)," he also said, "older, more advanced residents would also be intermixed so the actual population could be as high as 30–40." As the program grew, he wrote, "other houses could be added to form a sort of village city wide, state wide, national. A lofty goal but like any good thing that begins it will continue to grow.

"Oholah House is exactly that," he continued, "a house, a cross between a college dorm and a clinic. While attempts should be made to foster a casual dorm environment there should also be a system of very definate rules built around a structured goal orientated program." Moreover, "the house itself would be a renovated house or city apartment building obtained via auction or donation. As a building it would have all the requirements of every other building, insurance, water, electric, tellephone, and repairs would have to be maintained by Oholah House as a corporation. The Oholah Corporation would be an NPC [nonprofit corporation] in compliance with and subject to all NYS [New York State] laws."

In Part Two, Joel described the obvious need for Oholah to raise money. "As a non profit corporation the Oholah House Foundation Inc., will openly and unabashedly solicit monies and materials from any source," he wrote. "It is toward that goal of obtaining money the following proposals are aimed:

The Oholah Angel—the prostitute Angel
Why an angel because there is a little angel in all of us. It also represents a non-religious way, the resurrection of the soul, the individual soul that is inside all of us. The program inside Oholah House are designed to put each resident in touch with her own individual potential and show each of them possibly for the first time as an adult what that potential is, in real life and not some idealized one (that others have tied to impose on them). To each her own, as the saying goes.

Some will discover that they are good cooks, others artists, others caregivers, and workers of all types. Each resident should be allowed and encouraged to find and determine her own niche in life and spirit.

The Oholah Angel is also a symbol; something to rally around, an identity. It is also a logo a moving characterization (a cartoon) that can be exploited for fund raising and even commercial use on tee shirts, posters, bottons, pins, jewelry and the like. It is something that the public can easily identify with (a thing that seems to be a cultural necessity).

Joel also planned for a subsidiary fundraising NPC [nonprofit corporation] to be called Penitence Ink or Penitence Art. "Celebrities, writers, Artists, house relatives or their relatives or just about anyone could donate a short story, interview, or Artwork to be marketed by O.H.F.C. Inc to raise funds. Individual agreements in the form of contracts would allow for the percentage of proceeds to be donated or returned to the contributor or split between multiple charities. An Annual collection of short stories, essays, poems and writings could be published of collected works by residents, Alumni, and relatives, or a guest celebrity or two."

In addition, wrote Joel, "Artists could donate works to be reproduced and marketed, for example as Prints, Greeting Cards, coffee mugs, ect., could be packaged and sold in area stores or via mail order." By acting apart from OHF, "residents and alumni of Oholah House would be able to donate to the house and be able to keep portions of the proceeds for themselves to begin their new lives with." Also, "Penitance Art & Ink could employ Residents and alumni as a way of teaching job and employment skills. Thus a two fold purpose for both raising funds and creating jobs for the program itself. Marketable job skills are of paramount importance to the self sufficiency and survivability of Alumni. The important goal of the project is to foster a deep sense of self worth and independence to enable them to overcome lifes obstacles without being tempted the turn back to the life they left."

He also devised a plan where corporate sponsors could donate money, products, services, time, or job training. "Corporations could participate in job training programs by providing guest lecturers or temporary employment for Residents and Alumni," he wrote. "Donations could be of used office furnature, surplus supplies, copy machines, computers, and similar office items. Companies could donate time in the form of a service ie., printing. Corporate and individual donations could be from as little as dollars to as large as mega dollars. Levels could be [a] House—a major portion of a House annual budget. Suite—A portion of a single house."

Part Three outlined the support and structure, comprised of three components, "Reunion program, Sisterhood program [and] (Reality)," which Joel described as "the heart of the program its uniqueness that makes the House also a home."

The reunion program was integral because "family support is essential to recovery. Family is the foundation of a persons entity and without it to depend on for support, a person is off balance and unable to stand on ones own."

Joel also believed that "A buddy or sisterhood should be encouraged between New Residents and established Residents—Residents and Alumni—Alumni and Alumni. This is similar to an A.A. sponsor the only diffrence is that sisters have a common up bringing, a uniqueness from other families. All the Residents of Oholah House have the street life as a common parent along with the common scares of troubled childhoods. It is this common bond that forms a tighter union than a sponsership between strangers."

Crucial to the success of the sisterhood is homecoming, because "every Alumni is considered a resident for life in that the door is always open for returnies to come back for what ever reason. Life is a continual series of ups and downs and a person always needs to know that they can return Home. It is better that Alumni return home then to return back to a life of addiction or back to the streets."

The annual homecomings or reunions were of paramount importance and should be held on site, explained Joel, because "this would be a yearly way for those who need both believe and realize that they are not alone that others are living and succeeding in similar lives from a similar history and needs. It is a way of renewing freindships and strengthening support."

As grand as that all sounded, the real meat and potatoes of OHF was the "Motivation Room (Reality)." This was "unique to the concept of Oholah House," said Joel, "[in] that it was born of tragedies; those deaths form the core of the motivation to recover the future for the Residents and Alumni of the House. A shortened life is a realistic possibility of the life that the residents are trying to leave. Death can take on many forms, be it at the hand of a client who loses it, a pimp, a drug overdose or disease. The concept must be firmly implanted in a Residents mind that the Life is like one extreomly long suicide. Death should be used as a motivator, a form of scared Straight, it is fundemental to the program. Reality is what it is, it is base, tramatic, harsh. Reality should never be sugar coated it needs to be up front it should bring tears it should be rough. To accomplish this photographs should be used visits to hospitals even a visit to the morge. Even a chance for someone to meet a person like me to realize how ordinary and normal looking a person who is capable of causing great harm."

Calling Oholah House an "evolving work in progress," Joel said "to that end there is yet no conclusion." For that reason he kept the proposal "simple" to "serve as an outline a plan of the future." Without the foundation yet to be built, "it is far to early to begin to think of the paint and sparkle." Once the clients completed specific steps of their rehabilitative process under the tutelage of Joel they would become one of many Oholah Angels. Although Joel insisted he had no belief in God or the afterlife, he did not seem to find the term angel inconsistent.

Of course, one might question just what Joel knows about reality of any kind. He killed seventeen women, he had never been gainfully employed for any extended period of time, he suffered from an array of addictions and compulsions, and he was never self-sufficient. When it came right down to it, the only thing he ever did with any success was murder people. Now he wanted to run a halfway house for wayward women, as if he were a community-minded corporate head. While some might recognize his value as a speaker in warning prostitutes that no customer should ever be deemed completely safe, what business did he have serving as a mentor in their physical, mental, and spiritual recovery process?

When asked if his actions might be interpreted as a ploy to earn him better living quarters, a celebrity cult following, or acceptance by mainstream America, he simply shrugged his shoulders and said, "Why attempt to do this? Because everyone deserves a second chance and this, in some personal way, is an attempt to make up for those second chances that I took away. Oholah is an attempt to create a means by which others might not have theirs taken or lost. In comparison to the greater scheme of things this might not seem like much, but at least it is something. And it is all I know to do or can do at this time."

Joel's efforts caused a stir in some circles and he received some surprising support from others. "It's obviously well thought out," said Sidney-Anne Ford, executive director of the You Are Never Alone Project, a nonresidential treatment center for prostitutes in Baltimore. "This is a great thing he's working on. It's a pretty compassionate model for service. It makes me somewhat sad to think that because of his status, the needs of women might go unmet."

"Joel's a very bright person, that was very clear,"

said ADA Fred Klein, who so vigorously prosecuted him for the Bresciani homicide. "He's trying to help people, and I don't see why people shouldn't listen. If he's come to the conclusion that he wants to use his brain and help people, that's good. Maybe he hopes some day that people will see there's another side of Joel Rifkin. He's a very thoughtful—at times, sensitive—person. There's something very different about him. He just has that one flaw."

"I never saw anything that indicated he showed any remorse or feeling toward these people," countered ADA Michael Ahearn, who prosecuted Joel for the murders of Leah Evans and Lauren Marquez. "If he did, that's great. But I'm skeptical. If it happens, I think it would be an insult to the memory of his victims. I don't think he should be personally involved in it."

"It really doesn't matter to him if this organization ever comes to fruition," said Ray Pierce. "Joel will thrive on the development, production, and progress of the project. He couldn't care less if one or one hundred women utilize the place. This is just a manifestation of his need to control, to stroke his ego, to be seen in a positive light. He thrives on the media attention. As terrible as he was depicted during the court proceedings, I'm sure he thrived on that too."

Melissa Farley, the director of the Center for Prostitution Research and Education in San Francisco, said Joel's proposal addresses the three things women need most to turn their back on the streets: housing, drug treatment, and psychological treatment. But she also felt that the horrors of the Motivation Room are unnecessary because the women are living with those horrors every day. "It kind of speaks to the fact he doesn't get it," she said. "It shows he bought the argument that prostitutes enjoy doing it."

It seemed to me that this was the only way he knew to get back, in some vicarious way, to the streets that were no longer accessible to him. As the controversy raged on, Joel, in his solitary, windowless Attica cell, forged ahead in trying to make his concept a reality. Who better than he, he mused, could warn women about the dangers and the pitfalls of the streets? Who better than he could help women along the path to recovery? I asked Joel how anyone could believe that he'd be able to make such a transition without the benefit of therapy, without any genuine growth from the day he got arrested. He was asked if he ever truly saw himself as a decent, caring, considerate man.

"He likes to think he is now," he responded flatly. "But yeah, the perspective is 'yeah, he's a killer, he's a monster, lock him up forever.'"

20

JOEL'S PERCEPTION OF HIMSELF AS A

benevolent soul was not the only thing that surprised the public. He caused controversy in 1998 when he submitted twenty oils, colored pencil sketches, and watercolors to the Correction on Canvas Art Show and Sale in Albany, New York, the state capital. Inmate art work from prison facilities throughout the state is showcased for several days each April at a government building. Fifty percent of the sale price is immediately disbursed to the New York State Crime Victims Board, which was responsible for drafting the Son of Sam law that precludes state prisoners from profiting in any way from their crimes.

While the proceeds might be used to help provide physical therapy for the sufferers of an urban crime spree or as counseling for a rape victim, at least some of the money ultimately finds its way into the pockets of the artists. Half of the remaining fifty percent is put into the prisoner's administrative account, where it is used for the payment of court-mandated fees or restitution to victims. It may also be used for "gate money," which is provided to the inmates upon their release to find their way home, usually by bus. The remaining money, is funneled to the inmate himself and used for such penitentiary staples as art supplies, commissary junk food, reading material, toiletries, and cigarettes.

Especially charitable prisoners can donate their entire earnings to the Crime Victims Board. If they choose that option their work is given prime placement by being exhibited in a giant open area just inside the entrance rather than in the narrower rows that are alphabetized by institution toward the rear of the display area. While many artists were glad to get the added exposure and expressed a seemingly heartfelt need to give something back to society, cynical observers viewed their altruism as an attempt to garner a favorable review with the Parole Board.

As the most notorious prisoner in the state penal system, Joel, who chose not to donate all of his earnings, harbored no illusions about being granted clemency some day. Nor did he expect his nominal contributions to the Crime Victims Board to curry him any favor with prison officials. Left alone, with little more to do than reflect on his egregious past and a future of nothingness, Joel found some escape in his art work. "It is very therapeutic," he explained. "You tend to focus on what you're doing."

Like so much else about Joel, his paintings and drawings were a study in contradictions. Although his crimes were as ghastly as any in the annals of criminal history, his drawings offered little insight into the darkened spirit of his soul. What was clear, however, was that despite his being tucked away in prison for at least 203 years, Joel's personality, whether seen in a television interview or through his art work, still offended people who came in contact with him. Not only were people outraged that he had the audacity to participate in the art show, they were even more outraged that he could benefit as a result. One Brooklyn woman who visited the exhibit that year angrily told a reporter for New York *Newsday*, "I'm not interested in anything he would want to express."

While she might not have been interested, there was no shortage of people who were. Joel sold six pieces that year, which ranged from the tranquil to the macabre, for prices ranging from $27 to $81. One, entitled "Desert Rain," was a southwestern scene showing a cactus and a purple sky. "Water Lilies" depicted white lilies floating on a green background.

Another, "800's Angels," paid homage to the victims of the TWA Flight 800 crash, which had occurred a few months earlier off the coast of Moriches, a small town in eastern Long Island that was less than an hour's drive from Joel's childhood home and minutes away from the desolate graves of Lauren Marquez and Leah Evans. It depicted a woman weeping on the beach as angels hovered overhead. Again, I was reminded of Joel's steadfast disbelief in the afterlife. When I pointedly asked him if he even thought such places as heaven or hell existed, his response was an immediate and emphatic "No!"

The religious imagery recurred in his picture called "A Guardian's Failure," which showed a human foot with a medical examiner's toe tag attached to it. Nearby was a weeping angel, its head bowed. Whether or not Joel was referring to the failures of his own parents or the parents of his seventeen victims is unknown. Joel skirted the question.

Joel was unmoved by the controversy that continued to envelop him. "At the show six of my paintings sold," he said. "No one forced them to buy them, and yes, the sale was controversial. The bottom line is that I was able to raise eighty-two dollars and fifty cents for the Crime Victims Fund."

In 1999 a man who worked in the camera and radio division of the State Assembly spent twenty-seven dollars on one of Rifkin's untitled paintings. Signed J. Rifkin, it depicted a plane and a duck. When informed by a reporter who the actual artist was, the buyer looked stunned and deflated. "I didn't realize it was him until I bought it," he said. "Now I'm not so sure I'm going to hang it up."

Joel submitted paintings to the 2000 exhibit, which I attended, and many of his entries were mystifying. Two cuddly, adorable panda bears stood side by side in "The Lover and the Bored," while two ducks squared off in "Ninja Face-off." Many other pictures showed big animals acting as mentors or protectors to little animals. There was a family of prairie dogs, an adult zebra hovering over a baby zebra, a familial pack of elephants of all sizes, and a tough but tender-looking canine boxer acting as a sort of sentry to an inquisitive butterfly in "Hurruhh?!"

A painting called "Domes Are for Wimps" showed a battered but seemingly unbeaten and unbowed football player, his face creased by pain, bad weather, and even worse luck. Although Joel insisted that his father was not his inspiration for the drawing, there is much evidence to the contrary. When I asked what the drawing meant to him, he got the same bemused look he always did when speaking about his dad, and he conceded the drawing was of a player on the Green Bay Packers, the team he and his father watched most often together when he was a child.

"That was the old Green Bay," said Joel in describing the drawing. "They had two conditions that I remember as a kid: mud soup or frozen ice. That's like insane football. [They would say] we'll play in a frozen field or we'll play in a wet, muddy field because they refused to build a dome. You got the teams in Florida playing in domes [and] you can't get nicer weather than Florida."

Pressed to explain a possible correlation between the drawing and his father's football prowess, as well as Ben's fierce loyalty to athletic traditions, Joel blurted out in an almost defiant manner, "Oh no, he didn't like dome football as a fan. He liked mud ball games too."

Joel was both thrilled and surprised by his artistic success but he seemed unaware that his notoriety had anything to do with it. "Any inmate could attempt to sell paintings there so I put a few paintings in, [and] all of a sudden it makes the Albany paper," he said. "It goes on a wire service. I saw versions of it in three different papers; someone sent me an Internet version of it. That woke me up to [the fact that] it's five years after the fact and there's still a kernel of [interest]."

It was obvious that Joel was as adept an artist as he was a killer, but oddly enough most of his drawings offered little insight into his seemingly twisted mind. Art is said to offer a glimpse into the soul, but Joel's drawings provided no explanations of his soul. They did not begin to tell the story of the quiet, unassuming man who lived with his parents throughout most of his adult life, had few girlfriends, and like so many others—most of whom never fantasize about killing much less commit murder—was besieged by an array of idiosyncrasies and neuroses.

Only two other drawings seemed to delve into the dark side that Joel kept secret for so long. One, a noirish untitled pencil sketch, showed the unnerving face of an obviously troubled young woman, while the other, "Lady in Black," depicted a woman adorned in sadomasochistic garb looking as vulnerable as she did willing. She seemed to possess both a whore's hardness and a waif's innocence. "She was in one of the biker magazines that circulate in here," he modestly explained. "I was looking for high contrast for black and white, so that the wet face where the girl is looking down is just a tight head shot. Nothing in particular in that."

Whether he realized it or not, such drawings provided forensic fodder for psychiatrists, mental health experts, social workers, criminologists, and journalists, myself included. Could she have really been a masturbatory replica of his favorite victim, I wondered? Or a composite of all of them?

I was worried that she wouldn't on page
[...] she suffered almost without pain. Had I
[...] would deprive Joel the [...] either one of
[...] Being that with another man

It did not take long to realize he was just as
comfortable talking to me about his career as he
was talking to Joel about motorcycles. Talking
and experiences I found among the useful not as well as
a others that followed, described about his own
[...] an inner temperament may [...] for a
[...] but I did was part in the research the
[...] which was telling an insider's tale is
[...] the hope of the man has almost good quality

OVER A TWO-YEAR PERIOD I RECEIVED
countless letters from Joel, including Christmas
cards and a congratulatory greeting after I became
a father for the first time. He even called collect a
few times. Once, when I wasn't home, he had a
five-minute conversation with my wife that she
described as pleasant. I first visited Joel at Attica
in September 1999, while on assignment for *Details* magazine. Accompanying me was photographer Chris Buck, who found Joel to be as likable
and outwardly harmless as I did.

Through my letters Joel learned how seriously I
had taken him as a photographer and how disturbed I was that he threw away such limitless potential. But I think my presence at Attica brought
home to him just how much he'd lost. I asked him

if the visit caused him sorrow, regret, or envy. "Sure," he answered almost whimsically. "Had I not had certain problems, I could be either one of you today, doing this with another inmate."

It did not take long to realize he was just as comfortable talking to me about his crimes as he was talking to Buck about camera angles, lighting, and techniques. During the initial visit, as well as at others that followed, he talked about his grisly crimes in an oddly resonant manner. Never for a second did I feel as if I was in the presence of a madman, which was chilling in its own right. As the narrator of his own barbarism, Joel seemed more like a confused, emotionally underdeveloped man than anything else. Although Dorothy Otnow-Lewis, a renowned psychiatrist and author of the best-selling book *Guilty by Reason of Insanity*, was quoted as saying Joel was "crazy as a bedbug," I never saw that aspect of his personality, even when he talked about things that only a crazy man could think of. Perhaps his institutionalization, as well as the variety of medications he was taking for the first time in his life, was keeping him on an even keel.

Joel reminded me of a youngster raised on cartoons who had become so desensitized to violence that he could no longer differentiate between the real thing and what he viewed on Saturday morning television. I had elicited confessions from teenage killers to terrible crimes, only to see them sleeping soundly in their cells shortly afterward. But many of them seemed even less childlike than Joel. While they were not completely out of touch with reality, some of them expected me to believe a revolver could be fired without the trigger being pulled, or that people could be shot point blank by accident. It was not much different from Joel saying he killed simply because he could not suppress the urge. As I tried desperately to see Joel as an evil and cunning predator, he just seemed more emotionally oblivious than anything else.

But it was clear that intellectually he knew right from wrong. He understood that he took all those lives and that the women weren't coming back. Still I could not call him a demonic being, even though his actions certainly warranted that designation. Could it be that I was losing my forensic touch or the professional emotional detachment that had enabled me to become a successful detective and journalist? Was I somehow getting sucked into his web of deceit?

Because Joel had no other form of regular entertainment or emotional release in his life, I assumed he found all the pandemonium surrounding his killings thrilling. "Chaos is a very exciting time," he agreed. "So was the whole trial stage an exciting time."

Asked how he could live with the daily memory

of all the horror he had perpetrated, Joel was at first pensive, then expansive, in his explanation. I was eager to learn if the memories caused him revulsion, sadness, regret, sorrow, or perhaps even longing. "It's like remembering a car crash, very stark," he said. "[The memories] get pushed back after a while. Whenever they pop up, I try to bury them again. It's not a pleasant thing to have hanging around."

As I probed deeper Joel did not grow the least bit uncomfortable. For him, most things were simple, black and white. He rarely became animated or the least bit convivial. "So, number five popped into your head this morning?" I asked. "How long did it take to pop out?"

"It's still there because we're still talking about it," he responded. "But before I leave [the visitation room], it'll be back where it's supposed to be, back in, you know, buried, forgotten about. Generally, each day some kind of memory will come up. I really try not to let them linger. When an athlete talks about a great moment, he's happy, that's his whole career, to get the touchdown or home run. With this, there's no pride, there's no joy, there's no happiness. It's just, yeah, I did that."

Even as I listened to him claim the contrary, I know there was no way Joel was telling the truth about deriving no sense of joy or accomplishment from his horrific actions. If he didn't, why did he compare his murders to the athletic achievements that always eluded him as a youngster? It was increasingly obvious that the murders were the only highlights in an otherwise uneventful, nonachieving life. Not only were the experiences tremendously exciting, they transformed him from a hapless, fumbling loser to someone capable of arousing the passions of others. For a guy who spent a lifetime as a failure, being a murderer gave him three things he thought he could never obtain: an identity, a place in history, and a lifetime supply of fuel for his narcissism.

If nothing else, Joel should consider himself blessed to be able to live with any degree of internal peace. He is never cursed with nightmares or even an ounce of guilt or shame. As I listen to him speak, I desperately want to believe he is insane but firmly believe in my head and my heart that he is not. Although I am not a doctor, my police experience has given me enough insight into the human psyche to determine with some accuracy if someone is sane or not. But I wonder how someone sane could immerse himself in such insanity, especially when there was no evidence of antisocial behavior prior to the killings. How could he now reflect on his vile actions without being crippled by guilt and consumed by shame? By his own admission he knew exactly what he was doing before, during, and after each of these murders.

"The initial wave of doctors were trying to fit me into that case study box," said Joel. "It's like a round peg square hole type of thing. You can jam it in there, but it just doesn't [fit]."

The only real grudge he seems to harbor is against Dr. Dietz, whom he described as "a hired gun with such disdain for criminal defendants" that he was incapable of displaying any objectivity. He insists that Dietz did not play fair. "When Dietz was trying to put me in a corner with his predisposed thing, [he believed] these were sexually exciting periods, [that the memory] heightened the whole sexual thing and the whole orgasm thing," said Joel. "But there were other times I couldn't perform at all, couldn't maintain an erection or anything. Just nothing. So that doesn't fit what he wanted, so he dismissed it.

"What he likes to do is alienate the jury," he continued. "He testified at the [Arthur] Shawcross [trial], he testified at the [Jeffrey] Dahmer [trial]. He was gonna do the penalty phase for Susan somebody [Susan Smith], who drove her two kids into the lake [in South Carolina]. He was supposed to be on the penalty phase for the Unabomber. This is what he does. He travels the country and a technique of his is to get the jury disgusted."

Joel said he told Dietz the same version of the story he told me about Julie Blackbird: that he considered having sex with her corpse but decided not to. "I told it to Dietz exactly that way," he said angrily. "He left a few words out of it, labeled me a necrophiliac, told the jury that, and basically had them go *eeeww.*"

Dietz got Joel even more disgusted by saying he had a propensity for starting fires, even as a grade schooler. Nothing, insisted the admitted killer, could be further from the truth. "I think almost every child has some fascination with fire," he said. "And I had a chemistry set with a Bunsen burner. One time I was heating something, it got out of control, and the table cracked. In what I learned later about [David] Berkowitz, he used to set Dumpsters on fire and watch the police [and fire department] come. That goes beyond the fascination with fire. But you outgrow it. I outgrew it. Kids go through these stages. There's the dinosaur stage, then there's the I-wanna-be-an-athlete stage. Every kid goes through these progressions."

I was still having difficulty reconciling the Joel I knew in college and the killer who sat before me. Sure, I had heard graphic descriptions of his misdeeds, but I had also once seen him as a young man so much like myself. Adding to my ambivalence was the fact that in some small way—as hard as it is to believe—I actually liked him. But the sheer repugnance of his actions made it impossible to remain emotionally dissociated and completely objective. Those difficulties were only exacerbated after the birth of my daughter. For a time I began to take his crimes personally.

Every time I looked into the sweet, vulnerable, and trusting eyes of my beautiful baby daughter, I imagined Joel's seventeen victims at the same period in their own lives. Long before they were swallowed up by the vulgar temptations of the streets, their smiles were equally infectious, their futures filled with the same degree of innocent optimism. They too beamed proudly when speaking their first words, they too looked into the eyes of their mothers as if they were staring at God, and they too tried valiantly but vainly to keep their eyes open until the end of an enthralling bedtime story.

Still, I believed that deep inside Joel beat the heart of a desperate child screaming for help. While most people did not care about what he was thinking, much less what he had to say, I did. I had seen the home movies of him joyously pedaling a tricycle and reveling in his parents' company. At one point, Joel was every bit the carefree, curious, and innocent child that my daughter is now. But all the years of systematic emotional and physical abuse had reduced his self-image to the point that he felt totally unworthy of respect, friendship, or even love and protection, the natural birthright of all children.

A strong voice kept telling me there was an intrinsic link between us, a reason why we were brought together in the first place and reunited twenty years later. Why, I kept asking myself, did I have this desperate need to peer into Joel's psyche to find answers to questions I didn't even know about my own past? By examining the path he had taken, would I somehow feel better about the one I had chosen? Did I get reassurance or validation because he had failed at the game of life while, on paper at least, I had not? Was I just feeling guilty about the wonderful life I had created for myself, and reviving the past to make it seem all the more real to me?

Desperate for answers I contacted Elias Samas, the president of the Queens Graphoanalysis Center in New York City. A certified graphoanalyst, or handwriting expert, for twenty-five years, Samas, who is also a psychotherapist, had completed undergraduate and graduate studies at Columbia University and once served as the president of the New York chapter of the International Graphoanalysis Society. While most handwriting experts are employed by attorneys to discredit or authenticate documents, Samas, who only performed that service for about twenty percent of his clients, was one of the few analysts who did personality profiles based on a subject's writing. Although many of his clients were employers looking for insights into prospective employees and men and women checking out prospective mates, he regularly testified for firms, corporations, and individuals in state, federal, and civil courts.

Fluent in English, French, Greek, and Arabic, Samas could provide documentation and reports in all of those languages. In the mid-eighties he was even hired by the *National Enquirer* to analyze Frank Sinatra signature samples from 1940, 1951, 1965, and 1982. "Many people tend to become bossier and more narrow-minded over the years, but with Frank Sinatra it's just the opposite," he said. "Sinatra's handwriting reveals he was more domineering, close-minded, and secretive when he was young. But now that he's matured, he's more honest, open-minded, and talkative."

Even though I did not know Samas personally, I did know of his reputation as the premier personality profiler in the New York metropolitan area. My plan was to take a generic page from Joel's Oholah proposal, one that offered no indication of who the author was or what he had done. I would then copy the page word for word myself, with the same misspellings and grammatical errors, make photocopies of both, and have Samas examine them.

"I could give you at least thirty interpretations on the different ways people write the letter *T*," he explained. "A short *t* usually shows an independent character. A low crossbar on the letter indicates low self-esteem, while a crossbar in the middle of the up stroke indicates a person with practical goals in life. A crossbar at the top of the letter usually shows a person with visionary goals who will plan rationally to reach those goals. But if the crossbar is above the letter it indicates goals and dreams beyond the person's reach. But the person may have strong enough willpower to succeed if the crossbar is thick and bold."

After agreeing on a fee, I sent Samas the text. I was designated subject number one; Joel was number two. While Samas pegged neither of us as a killer, he made it clear that if he was to guess which one of us was involved in criminal activity it would have been me. That didn't exactly surprise me because I have always believed that anyone can have evil or depraved ideas but that through awareness and knowledge most of us can circumvent those occasional thoughts.

"The two prominent features in the handwriting of this person are his impulsive nature and his temper," he wrote about me. "People with such characteristics tend to act first and think later. Such features act as negative elements in a person's life. Another feature which intensifies impulsivity is his lack of attention to details. The cluster of the above three characteristics acts as a reducing factor in the person's dealings with others. A job requiring close attention to details may not have the best results in the hands of person [one]."

Furthermore, wrote Samas, I was "aware of my shortcomings and trying to control [my] impulsivity and temper." Plus, he said, I could "occasionally demonstrate low self-esteem and yield to others' opinions, [but] despite his reducing characteristics he is frank and has intuition, which could be an asset in reducing the negative effect of temper and procrastination."

Samas's observance of my temper was based on the way that I angled my letters far to the right of their baseline. My lack of attention to detail was determined by the fact that I dotted none of the *i*'s or *j*'s in my writing. My awareness of my shortcomings was shown by the curved *t* bars, which he said looked like the writer was "holding an umbrella to protect their self-esteem." Moreover, because my *t* bars were very low in relation to the *t* stems, I did not deal well with the abstract, meaning philosophy, science, and religion. Samas also said I was "optimistic" as a writer, but had "no creativity."

With Joel he saw no volcanic temper, no ominous rumblings beneath the surface. His assessment validated what I had been thinking about Joel all along, that he was not the least bit troubled by his actions. Samas viewed him as a person "with practical goals in life, an honest and frank person who is capable of taking criticism without being sensitive." This was determined by the fact that he placed his *t* bars in the middle of the letter. But, he warned, "a trait which may act as a reducing factor is his procrastination" as evidenced by the fact that he placed many of his *t* bars only on the left side of the stem. "He does not rush," continued Samas, but "pays attention to small details, as evidenced by his beautiful clear *o*'s and *a*'s," all of which were complete and clear with no loops. Joel's artistic talents were demonstrated by the flat horizontal line on his small *r*'s, and his lack of literary style was indicated by the fact that his *d*'s and *t*'s were "just straight lines with no loops." Moreover, Samas said Joel possessed "artistic features, [although] unlikely in the literary world."

Joel did fancy himself a writer, but even as an adult he still had great difficulty with spelling and grammar. While he had sound ideas and concepts, his writing resembled rambling diatribes more than anything else. While that probably could have been corrected with a few classes in rudimentary writing, or even a bit more concentration on his part, old habits die hard.

In many ways Samas's assessment substantiated and validated my own ambivalence toward Joel. It was refreshing to find that I was not the only one who saw him as an enigma. My temper was certainly more volcanic than Joel's, yet I could never imagine taking someone's life. But there were times I still had trouble accepting the fact that he had done so. Oddly enough, the only time I could clearly see Joel as a stone-cold killer was when I envisioned him feverishly drafting his Oholah proposal in the solitude of his Attica cell. That he could sit there pretending to care about these women, unencumbered by any sense of shame or guilt, riled me more than anything. While he might have claimed it was a result of a desire for redemption, whether he realized it or not, his sole motivation was to feed his runaway narcissism. Because his incarceration precluded him from killing any more women with his bare hands, he devised an alternative plan to kill them with "kindness."

22

IN THE SPRING OF 2000 JOEL WAS TRANS-
ferred from the solitary cell at Attica to the protective
custody wing at Clinton Correctional Facility in
Dannemora, New York. Deep in the heart of the
Adirondack Mountains, Clinton is 350 miles due
north of New York City, a short drive from the Canadian border. Soon after his arrival there, I received an
eight-page letter gushing over his good fortune at finally getting out of administative segregation. It was
as if he were an old friend embarking on a new career
in a strange city, enthusiastically relating all the details in his first letter to friends. Now that he was able
to make phone calls, I received several over the first
few weeks, but as he was no longer in segregation
and was enjoying his new social environment, Joel's
once frequent correspondence soon ceased.

During my one visit to Clinton, he told me of friendships he had developed and how his days were now filled with programs and classes. He is out of his cell ten hours a day instead of in it for twenty-three, has full commissary privileges, mess hall meals, and a radio and television in his cell. At Attica he could only hear the television, not see it. "I have pictures to go with the sound and my choice of channels," he jubilantly announced.

There is little threat of violence in the protective custody wing at Clinton because the inmates are so happy to be away from the perils of the general population. "That's what controls a lot of the behavior problems," explained Joel. "If you're a total screw-up, you don't stay long in the unit. Guys wanna stay as long as they can. They try and avoid transfers, try and avoid getting locked in. I think there's been two fights in the three months I've been here, [while] in [general] population there's been three stabbings in one week [in the yard alone]. So there's a big difference in contrast. They'll [inmates] swallow a lot more than they will in other places as far as pride, as far as anger, just to stay here."

He was taking a legal research class with sixteen fellow students that was taught by an inmate who had already completed the challenging curriculum. Once Joel completed the two-month course he would be eligible to take a state test. If he passed, he would earn a certificate enabling him to work in the law library of a New York State correctional facility. What was most apparent was that Joel, living within the artificial environment of a prison, was finally experiencing, in his own mind at least, what it was like to be normal. For the first time in his life he had structure, a goal he could not walk away from, and a social network of friends who were in no position to betray or abandon him. All of these factors seemed to agree with him in easily discernible ways.

Joel had finally found his utopia, a place where the disenfranchised and the dissociated were welcomed with open arms regardless of their past transgressions. Because none of his fellow inmates wanted to risk being relegated to general population, there was no dissension among them, even though they were all notorious criminals who had been convicted of what Joel referred to as "high profile newspaper, and skin crawl type of crimes." There was not even a need to strive for any degree of individuality because each and every daily decision was made by their captors. For Joel, whose life had always been ruled by his limitless phobias and fears, this was heaven on earth.

"I'm actually doing better in here," he said. "I have more of a social life than I had in the world. I enjoy myself more. The world was more stressful to me. Since I've been here, I've adapted to it and there's other pressures that I don't have. I don't have to please the boss. I don't have to please customers. I don't know, it's weird, I generally like it better. These places are supposed to be places of suffering, of punishment, [but] I'm getting along fine in here. I really don't climb the walls. For some people it's a lot less stressful not having to worry about where my next meal's coming from. Even choosing what the next meal is gonna be. There's no menu, we're just given it. There's no choice of where, there's no choice of when."

Joel had never been much of a rabble rouser to begin with, but living within the rules here brought him a sense of comfort and permanence he had never known. Never again would he be an outcast or the victim of incessant assaults on his character and person. Little did it matter that he was now living among sociopaths and psychopaths. In his new world he was accepted for exactly who and what he was. There was no bullying or backstabbing, no need for false pretenses or bravado.

He also found himself learning more about himself and others than he could have ever imagined. Not only was he finally comfortable being accepted by other men, he was even able to bond with them and not see himself as a freak in their presence. "Despite being on the track team I never really related to a group of men as men, the little quirky things that men do," he said. "Here I'm getting into that bonding, that socialization."

"Joel is now back in his eggshell," said Joe Piraino. "As long as the eggshell is intact, he is okay. He is probably more at peace with himself than he has ever been."

While Joel agreed with that assessment, he was still unsure about what the future held for him. "Each day is just one more day of recovery," he said. "Where I am right now is the best place for me. I don't think I'll ever do a homicide again. I have no plans to do it again."

Joel seemed surprised that other inmates were fascinated with him, but conceded that he was equally fascinated by some of them. "[Some are] either too intelligent or too friendly, amicable," he said. "The crime doesn't seem to fit the person." Told that many people would say the same about him, he just shrugged innocently. When I told him that I still found his actions difficult to fathom, his response was as animated as it was immediate. "So do I, and I was there."

Knowing how gung-ho he had been over the Oholah project at Attica, I asked how things were coming and he said it was on the back burner. No longer in solitary confinement, where he had little else to do, he had stopped his letter-writing campaign to the media. Joel seemed to have no more time for social activism. I told him how much the city had changed since his arrest; how two-term Mayor Rudolph W. Giuliani had instituted zero-tolerance policies that removed most of the criminal element from the streets in one fell swoop. As hard as it might have been for him to believe, the FBI had rated New York as the safest large city in the country for several years in a row. I told him that the police department was now using civil forfeiture laws to confiscate the vehicles of johns, and how former crash pads for hookers on some of his favorite strolls were now renting for three thousand a month.

I desperately wanted to believe I was reaching him, that there was a smidgen of humanity buried within the heart of the man who sat slouched before me. He smiled faintly as I described driving the entire length of his five-borough stroll on four separate nights and not seeing even one girl on the hustle. The cupboards were bare, I told him, the streets were now clean. While the world's oldest profession might be flourishing behind closed doors, finding a hooker on the street was about as easy as finding a live dinosaur in the zoo. By this time Joel's eyes were lifeless, his body slumped even more. Like the seventeen young women he murdered, the city he both loved and loathed was gone forever. "That's too bad," he said.

While that comment was revealing, a story he later relayed was even more telling. He recounted an incident that had taken place in the yard just days earlier. The way he described it, it was like three old friends sharing a smoke and discussing their darkest fantasies. Joel talked in the third person about himself, as if he were an invisible observer. "There's three of us talking, and one guy was asking, have you ever had the urge to kill somebody," he said. " 'Every now and then, that's my problem, I get this urge.' The third guy, he just starts laughing, he's just hysterical. He calms down, points to the other guy [Joel], and says 'do you know who he is?' "

Joel could not contain his own laughter as he told me this story. It was as if he completely missed the fact that he was the subject of the punch line, and that people like Barbara Jacobs, Mary Ellen DeLuca, Yun Lee, and his other victims had been reduced to nothing more than figments of someone else's vivid imagination and the basis of a sick joke. Suddenly his face turned serious, almost introspective. "It's a very weird feeling to be in a conversation like that," he said.

After all that I had heard from the mouth of the monster, I still cannot fathom why that story had such a chilling effect on me. Although my demeanor remained staid and my face focused, a chill raced through my body with the swift jolt of a cattle prod. Maybe Joel was crazy after all.

Index

Visit
❖ Pocket Books ❖
online at

....

www.SimonSays.com

....

Keep up on the latest new
releases from your favorite
authors, as well as author
appearances, news, chats,
special offers and more.

SIMON & SCHUSTER
A VIACOM COMPANY
www.SimonSays.com

Pocket
Books

2381-01